"*The Tenant Class* mal
against the idea of a ho
tem as one fundamenta
landlords. Tranjan provi
of tenant organizing in Canada, reminding us that resistance is
possible and ongoing. This book explodes entrenched myths
about renters and landlords and will change the way many people
understand the injustice of the housing system."

—Leslie Kern, author of *Feminist City* and
Gentrification Is Inevitable and Other Lies

"From now on, every time someone tells me that we just need to
build more housing, I'll tell them to read *The Tenant Class*. Then
let's talk about the realities of housing justice in this country.
Tranjan offers a powerful rallying cry against the struggles tenants
face and the organizing required to push for needed solutions."

—Mike Morrice, Green Party of Canada,
Member of Parliament, Kitchener Centre

"*The Tenant Class* cuts through the carefully crafted myth that
those in economic and political power are seeking fair solutions
to a mysterious 'housing crisis.' People who rent the homes they
live in are up against a system that has been developed to serve
the profit needs of landlords, developers, and bankers. In the face
of this, tenants must draw on their own rich history of resistance,
challenge that power structure, and fight for their own rights and
interests."

—John Clarke, former organizer with the Ontario Coalition
Against Poverty, Packer Visitor in Social Justice,
York University

"This isn't just another book about housing policy. *The Tenant
Class* is a rallying cry for anti-colonial and anti-capitalist tenant
organizing, replete with stories of struggle from the late 1800s
in Prince Edward Island to recent rent strikes in Parkdale and in
Hamilton. This is a must-read for anyone interested in building
working-class solidarity and achieving housing justice for all."

—Fred Hahn, President of CUPE Ontario

THE TENANT CLASS

Ricardo Tranjan

The Tenant Class
© 2023 Ricardo Tranjan

First published in 2023 by
Between the Lines
401 Richmond Street West, Studio 281
Toronto, Ontario · M5V 3A8 · Canada
1-800-718-7201 · www.btlbooks.com

Every reasonable effort has been made to identify copyright holders. Between the Lines would be pleased to have any errors or omissions brought to its attention.

Library and Archives Canada Cataloguing in Publication
Title: The tenant class / Ricardo Tranjan.
Names: Tranjan, J. Ricardo, author.
Description: Includes bibliographical references and index.
Identifiers: Canadiana (print) 20220454566 | Canadiana (ebook) 20220454647 | ISBN 9781771136228 (softcover) | ISBN 9781771136235 (EPUB)
Subjects: LCSH: Rental housing—Canada. | LCSH: Housing policy— Canada. | LCSH: Landlord and tenant—Canada. | LCSH: Apartment dwellers—Canada. | LCSH: Landlords—Canada.
Classification: LCC HD7288.85.C2 T73 2023 | DDC 363.50971—dc23

Cover and text design by DEEVE

Printed in Canada

We acknowledge for their financial support of our publishing activities: the Government of Canada; the Canada Council for the Arts; and the Government of Ontario through the Ontario Arts Council, the Ontario Book Publishers Tax Credit program, and Ontario Creates.

There's no such thing as neutrality. The people who use that label are people who unknowingly, for the most part, are dedicated to the support of the status quo.
—MYLES HORTON & PAULO FREIRE,
We Make the Road by Walking

CONTENTS

CONTENTS

INTRODUCTION

The Housing Crisis That Isn't

In a news article titled "The middle-class housing crisis," the *Toronto Star* warns that "if rent control were suddenly to cease, many families would suddenly be confronted by the danger of eviction or the necessity to find other accommodation because they could not afford to stay where they were."[1] An investigative news story in *Maclean's* contends the "housing crisis," which "shows no immediate signs of easing," is fuelling tenant organizing across the country.[2] In Quebec, *Le Devoir* reports on a press conference organized by tenant committees demanding provincial investment in affordable housing.[3] A commentary published in a BC magazine argues that "we must have more homes and we must have them at prices people can afford to pay."[4]

For many readers, these stories sound like a random selection of the last week's news. They could have been. The "housing crisis" is a recurring topic in Canadian media, with hardly a week going by where we do not hear new and daunting findings about how unaffordable housing has become. It is also a dominant theme in public policy circles, where "housing crisis" comes up regardless of the topic of discussion. Never mind the many podcasts, conferences, articles, and reports on the "housing crisis." All of this fuss conceals the fact that political struggle over housing is old news. The *Toronto Star* article is from 1950, the *Maclean's* story appeared in 1969, the Montreal press conference took place in 1980, and the BC commentary dates back to 1911. More importantly, the problem with all of this crisis talk is that there is no actual "housing crisis." That's right—there is no crisis.

The word crisis suggests something that is infrequent, surprising, and widely undesirable; something that leads to dire consequences unless it is brought under control. The United Nations defines a humanitarian crisis as "an event or series of events that represents a critical threat to the health, safety, security, or well-being of a community or other large group of people usually over a wider area." Examples include pandemics, natural disasters, and war. An International Monetary Fund study defines a financial crisis as "an amalgam of events, including substantial changes in credit volume and asset prices, severe disruptions in financial intermediation, notably the supply of external financing, large-scale balance sheet problems, and the need for large-scale government support." In fewer words: countries gone bankrupt.

It is fair to expect governments to act with resolve when dealing with real crises, swiftly deploying the personnel and resources needed to stop the bleeding. COVID-19 was a health crisis, and governments did what they did to contain the spread of the virus. Financial crises like the 2008 economic meltdown are met with prompt and costly government measures. The Russian invasion of Ukraine prompted a speedy, large-scale response from several countries and international organizations.

In contrast, Canada's "housing crisis" is a permanent state of affairs that harms people in, or in need of, rental housing; roughly one-third of the country's households. The other two-thirds own homes whose values rise much faster than other investment options. New homeowners may face high housing costs, but mortgage payments are accompanied by long-term growth in their personal wealth. Landlords, real estate investment firms, and developers operate in a stable and lucrative business environment. Even 2020—the first year of the pandemic when entire sectors of the economy were shut down—was a good year for the industry.[7] Banks and other mortgage providers create money, lend it, and charge interest on it. If that wasn't already a sweet deal, the federal government assumes a share of the risk of these mortgages so that banks can make easy money worry-free.

A housing system that serves all but one group is not in a state of crisis; it is one based on structural inequality and economic exploitation. For some readers, "exploitation" may sound too harsh a term. Renting properties is not only legal but morally acceptable, and some people argue landlords help tenants by providing them with a place to live. In the political economy tradition that informs this book, exploitation has a specific meaning; it refers to a group or class of people appropriating an unfair share of the fruits of the labour of another class. The classic example is workers and bosses.

The highest paid CEOs in Canada earn the equivalent of the annual income of average workers in just one morning.[8] People need to work, and if the jobs available are low-paying, they have no choice but to accept them. The wages these workers take home represent but a small portion of the total value of their work; executives and shareholders pocket most of that value. This is legal and widely accepted, which doesn't mean it is not exploitation. On the contrary, it is exploitation because laws, institutions, and moral norms allow some people to enrich on the backs of others. Unless tightly regulated, labour markets enable exploitation.

So does the rental housing market. Unlike most services and commodities, the price tag on rental units has no real relationship with the cost of providing housing. Rents are determined by "what the market will bear," as economists say. Even if a property has been paid for three times over (by previous tenants), landlords can charge well over the cost of maintaining that unit if that's what similar units are going for in the market. If the financial plan for a new building is to recover costs over 20 years, but the market squeezes more out of tenants than initially forecasted, the result is higher profits sooner than expected, not cheaper rents. The question is never if the rental property will generate profit; but rather, how much profit and how soon. The business is stable and lucrative because people have to live somewhere. If the cheapest available option takes the lion's share of their incomes—as with a third of tenant families—they have to take it.[9] Laws, institutions like landlord and tenant boards, and moral standards permit and legitimize wealth accumulation through rent collection.

In the aftermath of the 2008 financial meltdown, rental properties became the target of investors and speculators unwilling to let a good crisis go to waste. The COVID-19 pandemic became an opportunity for landlords to evict tenants, who fell into arrears due to the economic shutdown, and hike up rents. Government actions in recent years included partial cancellation of rent controls, wage freezes, the use of excessive force in the clearing of homeless encampments, the fast-tracking of evictions through virtual hearings, and the failure to protect people living in multi-tenant housing. The air feels heavy. But none of this is fundamentally new, or unexpected.

The purpose of the rental market is not to ensure the highest possible number of families is securely housed. The purpose of the rental market is to extract income from tenants, and as far as this goal is concerned, it works like a charm!

———————

This distinction between a "housing crisis" and a rental market that enables exploitation has practical implications. How we talk about these issues shapes what we conceive as possible and desirable responses to them. A "housing crisis" suggests the need for a technical solution and coordination between various stakeholders, all of whom desire the same outcome: the end of the crisis. Nobody is at fault. Politicizing the issue is unhelpful. We need win-win solutions. The right policy mix, backed by adequate government funding, is the only way forward; it would benefit everyone. This is, by far, the dominant view of how to deal with housing issues in Canada.

In this perspective, the market itself is never the problem. If rents go through the roof, working families cannot afford modest units, and parents have to choose between paying rent and putting food on the table, something is off with the rental market; it is not working as it should. Real estate lobbyists and some housing experts argue the problem is that supply is not catching up fast enough with demand. If we build more housing, the argument goes, people will have more choices and rent will be cheaper. The main problem with this "supply-side" argument is that it is not true.

In Economics 101, students learn the law of supply and demand, wherein prices fall if supply exceeds demand. The real world is more complicated, and that is particularly true for housing markets. There are many reasons for not treating housing as a market that arrives at an optimal balance.[10] The most important is that land, on which housing is built, is a fixed resource. We cannot produce more of it (though we can make better use of urban land). Highly desirable land—be it downtown Toronto building lots or prairie farmland—is fixed in quantity and scarce. There is little of it. Those who own it have the upper hand.

Another important difference between real-world rental markets and the law of supply and demand taught in Economics 101 is that housing is not bananas. Bananas spoil quickly, so it is in the interest of sellers to get rid of them, even if for a lower price than initially expected. Housing increases in value over time; someone holding onto an empty apartment in Vancouver is making lots of money in absolute terms, even if comparatively less money than if the apartment was rented. When a new tenant agrees to pay a higher rent for years to come, the waiting pays itself off in a few months, and the rest is profit. The correlation between the supply and price of rental housing is much more complicated than the proponents of "supply-side" arguments make it out to be.

For example, proponents of the "supply-side" argument frequently point to low vacancy rates as an indication that supply is low, which drives rents higher. During the COVID-19 pandemic, the national vacancy rate went up from 2 percent to 3.2 percent, a 60 percent increase. What happened to rents? They, too, went up, by 3.6 percent. In the City of Toronto, vacancy rates more than doubled between October 2019 (1.5 percent) and October 2020 (3.4 percent). What happened to the average rent in the city? It rose by 4.7 percent.[11] A Canada Mortgage and Housing Corporation (CMHC) report explained that, in hot markets like Toronto and Montreal, landlords chose to wait longer to fill vacancies or offered one-time rent discounts over lowering rents.[12]

In 2021, a prominent housing expert, Steve Pomeroy, demonstrated that "between 2006 and 2016, Canada added 1.636 million households and built 1.919 million new homes . . . almost 30,000 extra homes were constructed each year compared to the increase in the number of households."[13] And yet, housing prices and rents went up at a neck-breaking speed during those years. Neither Pomeroy nor I contend that Canada has enough housing or that additional supply would not be beneficial.[14] The point is that supply alone will not solve the problem.

Why, then, are "housing crisis" and "supply-side" arguments so prevalent? Canadian political economist Robert Cox famously said, "theory is always for someone, for some purpose."[15] He was criticizing studies that take the existing social order and institutions as a given. Problem-solving theories, as he called them, don't ask how things came to be, who benefits from the way things are, or whether things could be different. Instead, the focus is on smoothing out any troubles with the existing institutions. By not only accepting but helping to troubleshoot the current order, problem-solving theories legitimize and entrench the status quo. While priding itself on being value-free and offering practical solutions to concrete problems, this type of research serves the interests of those who are comfortable with the way things are and would rather avoid substantive changes.

A lot of housing research adheres to this problem-solving approach, and in doing so, it serves the interests of the real estate industry. If we believe lack of supply is the cause of lack of housing affordability, the solution is building more. If we build more but rents continue to go up, we must not be building enough. Build more, faster! How? Governments must provide financial and regulatory incentives to developers and remove rent controls, so that

~~landlords find the business more attractive. The "supply-side" argument serves a clear purpose: to sweeten the deal for developers and landlords. This argument has been made for decades; it has justified countless subsidies for the real estate industry, it has not lowered rents, and it will not go away either.~~ An argument that so directly supports the interest of an influential economic elite is not going anywhere, no matter how much empirical evidence is mounted against it.

The widespread use of "housing crisis" also helps to preserve the status quo. It reinforces the idea that Canada's housing system worked well at some point, but something unexpected happened, bringing about unseen and widely undesirable outcomes. That's not true. For a large share of the population, the housing system never worked, and the current state of affairs is making lots of people rich, like very rich. ~~It's not really a crisis if it has lasted more than a century and large sectors of the population wouldn't have it any different, is it?~~ Still, the housing debate in Canada centres on finding innovative, effective, evidence-based solutions to this so-called crisis. Years come and go. Public consultations lead to expert reports that call for more public consultations. The ultimate outcome of this policy merry-go-round is to conceal the power politics behind housing.

Cox also talks about critical studies that question the frameworks that problem-solving research conceals and legitimizes. This other type of research looks into social and power relationships, the origins of the prevailing order, and whether and how change happens over time. While problem-solving research digs into ever narrower aspects of an issue, critical research paints the big picture and situates the issue at hand. In addition to connecting parts and the whole, these studies link past and present, looking at sources of continuity and change. This historical context-ualization often leads to challenges to the notion that current issues are new and unforeseen. Critical studies also have a political agenda but don't pretend otherwise.

This book puts forward an alternative, critical perspective of the so-called housing crisis. It contends the rental market works as markets are supposed to work. Laws and law enforcement protect property rights over land dispossessed from Indigenous Peoples, creating private property and providing the basis for a housing market. In this market, landlords appropriate a large share of workers' incomes, accumulate, reinvest, and come back for more. They get wealthier every day while tenant families fall behind. There is no invisible hand hiking up rents and forcing tenants out. That hand is the hand of a landlord, resolutely extracting income from workers. Rents don't go up. Landlords raise rents.

From this perspective, the solution is political, not technical. The response to structural inequality is rebalancing power between social groups (or social classes) so that one can no longer exploit the other. Asking "pretty please" usually doesn't work. Bosses and landlords do not renounce profit and wealth. Historically, the working class made gains through organizing on the ground, pooling resources together, and amassing the power to confront bosses and demand better wages and working conditions. The same is true for the tenant class: its economic and political gains are the fruits of organizing, resisting abusive practices, and confronting landlords and the governments that side with them. It takes a struggle. It always has.

Knowledge is an important aspect of these struggles. Elites spend tonnes of money on producing and disseminating information and narratives that advance their interests, and they are successful at making their views sound

like common sense. The claim that building additional
rental housing will bring rents down is repeated daily by
news outlets because it suits the real estate industry. On
the other hand, the politicized perspective is largely absent
in the media and policy circles. It is found mostly in the
practice of tenant unions, *comités logement*, and other
class-based social movements. There is less written, and
said, and discussed about housing from this perspective,
and that's no accident. It is the elite successfully driving the
narrative.

As a senior researcher at the Canadian Centre for
Policy Alternatives (CCPA), a public policy think tank, I
regularly participate in policy debates with academics,
researchers in other institutes, and analysts in government.
I also frequently speak to the media about the "housing
crisis" and other policy issues. There is a time and place
for some problem-solving analyses, for trying to challenge
the narrative from within, but in my experience, that is not
enough. Growing up in the turbulent Brazil of the 1980s,
from an early age, I learned that concrete change follows
hard-fought political disputes. And in 15 years of academic
and applied research, I have never seen an example of elites
giving up power and wealth because the experts came
up with a bright idea. Ideas are nice, but it takes political power to move the needle. For this reason, progressive
research must directly support people at the frontline of
the struggle. They are the ones creating the conditions for
social change.

This book is written for tenants, with direct input from
tenant organizers, with tenant political goals and concerns
in mind. Its purpose is to provide these movements, and
anyone interested in rental housing, with a resource free
of the dominant, disingenuously apolitical housing policy
framework.

Following a brief overview of the concept of social class, I first look at the socioeconomic characteristics of tenants and argue they comprise a social class that is economically exploited. In a society where homeownership is the hallmark of a successful middle-class life, the tenant class is also up against myths and lies that denigrate its public image and hinder organizing efforts. While landlords extract ever more profits for the tenant class, Canadian society treats tenants as an inferior group.

Next, I focus on landlords, providing a typology of and estimate of the size of each group. Too often, landlords are conceived as individuals and families with modest incomes, and their financial well-being is juxtaposed against that of tenants. A closer look shows that the rental market is comprised mostly of wealthy families, profit-seeking business, and aggressive financial investors. This mischaracterization of landlords as struggling families and "mom-and-pop" shops is not accidental: it is a central plank in the depoliticization of housing.

Then, I turn to a well established Canadian tradition: tenant organizing. For a long time, tenants in Canada have organized to fight landlords, much as workers have organized to fight bosses. Detailing historical accounts and present-day struggles, their setbacks and victories, we see the different strategies of tenant movements. There are several ways to advance the historical, class-based movement for housing justice.

Finally, I contend that people concerned with housing justice should look at the alleged housing crisis for what it really is: a poorly regulated market that extracts income from working-class people and channels it to higher-income segments of Canadian society. And that's what poorly regulated markets do. The solutions are known. What is lacking is not data or ideas or sophisticated policies. An alternative, just housing system requires landlords and developers to give up high profits, which they won't consent to. It takes a struggle. And in this struggle, there are no win-win solutions. Tenant movements already know this, but policy folks and everyone else must also pick a side.

This book is the result of a collective effort. The CCPA put its organizational capacity behind this project and research agenda more broadly, and that is only possible because of our donors. The Catherine Donnelly Foundation provided the research grant that kick-started this work. Between the Lines offered it a home. And what a nice home it is. Tenant groups offered invaluable input on the original research proposal; written and oral accounts of their struggles have been an important source of knowledge and inspiration. Friends and colleagues provided trenchant feedback and continuing encouragement. Lastly, social and resistance movements of the past held the line where they could and kept alternatives alive for our political imagination, and for that, I'm always grateful.

CHAPTER ONE

Tenants, a Social Class

Governments decide how housing is built, renovated, used, rented, bought, and sold. Nothing *just is* when it comes to housing. From the height of an apartment building to the financing of it to whether tenants can smoke on their balconies, some people, at some point, decided it was going to be that way. Every decision brings benefits to some and losses and inconveniences to others. A single city council vote on a zoning bylaw can at once create new fortunes and ruin lives—and that is as political as anything gets. Yet, the high cost of housing is constantly presented as the outcome of invisible forces that governments haven't yet figured out how to arrest. The experts are on it, trying hard to find the right policy mix! But no magic policy bullet is ever found, and the only real outcome is the depoliticization of housing.

It happens with other issues. Take poverty, for example. In 2014, Toronto City Council directed city staff to develop a poverty reduction strategy in consultation with city residents. Thousands of people participated in online surveys, town hall meetings, and more than 100 small group discussions. City staff published consultation results and included much of what residents said in the strategy submitted for Council approval.[1] It was a good participatory process. Yet, the political mobilization the consultations

fuelled had all but died just a year later, and the strategy
delivered very little.[2] The development of a poverty reduction strategy helped to depoliticize poverty.

This is how it happened. During consultations, participants were asked to provide input on housing affordability, transit equity, food security, income security, and
city services. In town hall meetings, they had to choose a
table on one of these topics—a hard choice for many as
all topics were important and part of their lived experience. Whenever residents had the opportunity to speak or
write freely, their stories touched on a least a few of these
issues, and many named the people causing them harm:
the boss that pays too little, the landlord that charges too
much, the community housing provider that refuses to call
pest control, the premier that froze social assistance rates,
the mayor that chose to keep property taxes low and raise
transit fares, etc. But then city staff—I was one of them—
turned consultation input into dozens of initiatives that did
not explicitly name the cause of the problem, and assigned
them to one or more of the city's 30 divisions and agencies.
The people and processes creating poverty disappeared
during the policy development process. All of a sudden,
poverty was nobody's fault.

In contrast to this depoliticizing "complex policy"
approach that cuts issues into a thousand pieces, some
social scientists use the concept of social class to glue
the pieces back together and shine a light on the political
dimension of socioeconomic issues like poverty and housing
insecurity. Class analyses expressly name the people taking
too much, and those from whom too much is taken. They
explain how appropriation takes place, paying attention to
institutions that enable the rich and powerful to have their
way. Class analyses also look into how workers and other
subaltern groups resist and overcome exploitation. The

political power that leads to substantive change is achieved by connecting issues and uniting people with the same class interests, not segmenting them.

SOCIAL CLASS

First, the basics. What is social class? In the Marxian tradition, what determines people's social class is their relation to the means of production, defined as the physical and financial assets used to produce goods. Since Marx studied societies where manufacturing was or was becoming the principal economic activity, he focused mainly on two classes: the bourgeoisie, or capitalist class, who owned factories, machinery, and other productive assets; and the proletariat, or working class, who worked in those factories, providing the labour necessary to manufacturing. In capitalist societies, Marx argued, capitalists pay workers only a fraction of what their work is worth, appropriating the rest for themselves. Capitalists then reinvest profits in new activities that exploit yet more workers. The bourgeoisie accumulates wealth while the proletariat lives on subsistence wages.[3]

Over the years, scholars and militants have used the term "social class" in more than one way. Some authors use the term only when referring to the fundamental division that structures all social relations in a capitalist society, namely, wage labour. This strict focus allows scholars to advance a coherent body of knowledge. Other authors use the term more loosely, adapting it to their contexts and areas of interest. Prabhat Patnaik, an Indian economics professor involved in political debates in his country, defended the view that Marx's ideas should not be treated as concepts frozen in time but as tools in concrete analysis aimed at supporting emancipatory movements.[4] This book embraces the second approach. It applies the term to a critical division in society—tenants and landlords—but one that is admittedly not as structural as wage labour.[5]

In this book, we also deviate from the Marxian tradition in regard to land ownership. Before capitalist production and accumulation begin, communal land is converted into private property and the people who live off the land into wage workers, through a process Marx called primitive accumulation. Typically, a brutal process where "conquest, enslavement, robbery, murder, briefly force, play the great part."[6] Marx and conventional Marxism treat primitive accumulation as water under the bridge, a forgone process during the rise of capitalism.

Dene Indigenous Studies scholar Glen Coulthard disagrees. He calls attention to the "*persistent* role that unconceded, violent dispossession continues to play in the reproduction of colonial and capitalist social relations."[7] This book embraces this second view of primitive accumulation, and takes to heart Coulthard's warning that progressive political projects that advocate for communal ownership but ignore the injustice of colonial dispossession risk becoming complicit with the structures they oppose.

These caveats aside, the tenant-landlord relationship embodies many aspects of a class struggle. In Canada, it began with primitive accumulation in its worst form, genocide. Private property well established, society was then divided in two distinct groups. On the one side, tenants who have no choice but to engage in asymmetrical power relations to secure one of the most basic human needs, shelter. On the other side, a capital-owning class that extracts income from tenants and reinvests profit into additional rental units, which they again rent for more than what they are worth. Whereas tenants may have no savings after a lifetime of work, landlords steadily accumulate wealth. But this is also a history marked by resistance. Tenants unite, pool resources, amass political power and confront the landlord class.

ECONOMIC INJUSTICE

The economic exploitation of tenants hides in plain sight. The Canadian media regularly reports on fast-increasing rents, ballooning house prices, and cash-strapped families spending too much on housing. Politicians of all stripes speak about the issue and promise action. Governments and housing agencies conduct endless consultations on housing strategies. Housing advocacy groups and policy researchers repeatedly report on housing insecurity and high rents that drive financial insecurity. The rent is too damn high. Everyone knows it. And yet, nothing is done about it.

The way we talk about a problem matters. In housing debates, the key term shaping the conversation is "affordability." Everyday phrases include "housing affordability crisis," "lack of affordable housing," "the need for more affordable housing," and "government investment in affordable housing." These phrases are used to describe both high rents and high house prices. When it comes to high rents, the continuing use of "affordability" as the way to describe the problem serves to conceal profit-making. It confers an aura of blamelessness to the problem as if uncontrolled natural forces are driving rents up. The price of rent is not an intrinsic attribute of rental units but an exogenous factor determined by market relations. What renders rental units "unaffordable" are landlords who charge too much for them and governments that allow it to happen.

How problems are measured matters a great deal, too. The key measure in housing debates is the shelter-cost-to-income ratio. For tenants, shelter costs include rent and utilities. Income, in this case, means the total income of a household; the sum of what everyone brings in before taxes. By convention, and for no other reason, a household is considered in unaffordable housing if shelter costs consume 30 percent or more of their total income. (In housing debates in the post-war period, the threshold was 20 percent, but that shifted over the years, in the direction that benefits landlords).[8]

Statistics Canada and the CMHC regularly provide good quality data on shelter-cost-to-income ratios, feeding housing debates in public policy circles and the media. Researchers and news outlets of all political persuasions use this data. Be it in a Canadian Centre for Policy Alternatives (CCPA) blog arguing for stronger rent controls,[9] a C.D. Howe Institute article proposing rent insurance to shield landlords,[10] a policy brief proposing an eviction prevention plan during the COVID-19 pandemic,[11] or one of the several news stories about the financial insecurity of tenants,[12] the 30 percent affordability threshold is almost always part of the conversation. The problem with the widespread use of this measure is that it focuses on how much tenants pay, neglecting the other side of the equation, namely, how much landlords profit.

Official government documents also emphasize affordability and overlook the people pocketing high rents. Here are two examples. The City of Toronto lists "maintain and increase access to affordable rents" as one of the objectives of its housing strategy.[13] Almost all proposed actions to achieve this goal consist of providing financial assistance to renters so they can pass the money on to landlords. The strategy document touts the fact that "the City provides rent supplements directly to landlords to help eligible households to 'bridge the gap' between rental costs and the amounts that the households can actually afford to pay."[14]

The document also calls for an increase of highly inadequate social assistance rates in the province of Ontario so that social assistance recipients can pay rent.

The 109-page document does not mention the word "profit," except in the context of protecting and supporting not-for-profit housing providers. The impetus to provide financial assistance to low-income households is commendable, and the support for not-for-profit providers goes in the right direction. ~~That said, this document helps to perpetuate the problem by accepting high rents as a given and failing to mention stricter rent control as a more sustainable, long-term solution for the problem. Once again, the problem is presented as tenants not having enough income rather than acknowledging landlords are charging too much for rent.~~

The other notable example is the National Housing Strategy (NHS), released in 2017 amidst much political fanfare.[15] On the rental housing front, the original strategy included three main types of initiatives: financial support for new and existing social housing, funding for 60,000 new affordable rental units, and the target of "300,000 households provided with affordability support through the Canadian Housing Benefit."[16] Except for the support for social housing, the other two initiatives essentially channel money to developers and landlords. In this strategy and similar government initiatives, affordable rental units are defined as units where rents are kept at 80 percent of average market prices for a determined time, usually 20 years.

In other words, the government subsidizes the construction of rental units where rents can go up as fast as market prices, simply lagging behind 20 percent for a limited time. In turn, the housing benefit is a $200-a-month rent subsidy aimed at alleviating the burden of high rents on low- and moderate-income households; the strategy document presents it as "a new tool to fight the challenge of housing affordability."[17] A new tool with a known result: throwing money at landlords. The NHS also included a Solutions Lab initiative that offers "organizations with funding and expertise to help them solve complex housing problems,"[18] in other words, funding for more consultations and expert discussions about the "housing crisis." The 41-page document mentions "affordable" and "affordability" 86 times; the word "landlords" appears in only one paragraph. "Profit" is never mentioned, not once.

The 30 percent affordability threshold ignores the long-term financial security of tenants. The 20 percent-below-market standard for affordable rental units overlooks that housing markets are out of sync with the rest of the economy. The omission of landlords and their profit margins maintains a false veneer of neutrality in housing debates, reinforcing the idea of a technical problem for which no one is to blame. Let's examine other ways to look at these questions.

One way to contextualize rent prices with what is happening in the economy is to contrast rent increases with inflation. In 2001, the average rent for a two-bedroom unit in Vancouver was $920. Had rent increased at the same pace as inflation, the average rent would have been $1,310 in 2021. It was $1,830, or $520 higher. In 20 years, landlords managed to squeeze an additional $6,200 per unit, per year. That's no small change. Vancouver is the most severe example, but the same happened in cities across the country, including St. John's ($2,500), Halifax ($4,400), Montreal ($2,400), Toronto ($2,900), Winnipeg ($5,800), Saskatoon ($4,900), Edmonton ($3,900), and

Victoria ($6,000). Smaller cities like Hamilton ($3,900), Peterborough ($4,000), and Lethbridge ($2,000) have not been spared.[19]

In many cities across the country, rents also go up faster than income. Between 2006 and 2019, average rent for a two-bedroom apartment increased faster than after-tax income for tenant households in 14 out of 25 urban centres for which data is available (rents and incomes adjusted for inflation). In Saskatoon, for example, tenant income increased by 12 percent after subtracting inflation, while average rent went up by 60 percent above inflation (not including the shelter component of inflation and using provincial rates). In Hamilton, tenant income increased by zero percent after inflation while rents went up by 29 percent above inflation. In Victoria, tenants saw a 7 percent real income loss (it increased less than inflation), but rents pressed up all the same: 43 percent above inflation.[20]

Another clear way to show how landlords keep reaching deeper and deeper into tenants' pockets is to contrast the number of hours of work needed to pay rent. In 2020, a Peterborough tenant earning the average wage in that city needed 124 hours of work per month to afford a two-bedroom unit without spending more than 30 percent of their income on rent. In 2021, it took 161 hours, or 37 hours more. Peterborough was the worst example, but the CMHC found the same pattern in 20 out of 21 cities for which data was available. Other examples include Windsor (18 hours more), Halifax (12 hours more), Quebec City (5 hours more), Winnipeg (5 hours more), and Calgary (8 hours more). The authors concluded, "This data indicates that rent growth has exceeded wage growth in most centres over the same period."[21]

Even when tenant income increases at or above rents, above-inflation rent increases mean landlords take a bite at hard-fought gains. In Toronto, between 2006 and 2019, families earning the median income and renting an average-priced two-bedroom unit saw 24 percent of their real income gains going into the landlord's pocket. In Montreal, it was 20 percent. Smaller cities were not spared. In Saguenay and Abbotsford, rent took 13 and 14 percent of tenants' income gains, respectively.

Economic gains do not come easy. They are the results of collective workplace struggles, where workers organize, bargain, and strike for wage increases; of social movements that fight tooth and nail for minimum-wage increases; of tireless advocating for adequate income support programs like employment insurance, social assistance, and disability supports; of personal sacrifices made by individuals, parents, and children. Yet, everywhere in Canada, landlords grab a hefty share of those gains for themselves, pulling tenant families down.

———————

But it is not only landlords who pull tenants down. The capital-owning class as a whole does. Contrary to the overstated notion that a large share of tenants receive income support, tenants and homeowners have similar labour-force participation rates. Tenants are simply less remunerated for the work they do. They are overrepresented in low-paying jobs. Capital double-dips on tenant families by paying low wages from which high rents are subtracted.

The depoliticized affordability debate avoids both facts: landlords are the ones hiking up rents, and bosses pay too little. A CCPA study brought the two aspects of the problem together by showing the relationship between minimum wages and rents. Senior economist David Macdonald estimated the number of hours a week tenants need to work at the local minimum-wage rate to afford one- and two-bedroom apartments, in cities across Canada, without exceeding the 30 percent affordability threshold. In only three of the 36 metropolitan areas, a full-time minimum-wage worker can afford the average-priced one-bedroom apartment without working more than 40 hours a week, spending more than 30 percent of their income, or living with others to help pay the rent.[22]

Given high (and fast-increasing) rents compared to low wages, it should be no surprise that tenant families have little savings. Another CCPA study conducted at the out-set of the COVID-19 pandemic showed that 46 percent of working tenant households lived paycheque to paycheque.[23] Using data from the Statistics Canada's Survey of Financial Security, the study added up all their liquid assets, which is the term economists use for investment that can be eas-ily cashed out,[24] then calculated how many months' worth of savings tenant households had at their disposal. While countless media stories look at young families struggling to save for the down payment on a house, this seems to be a concern for a small share of tenant households. For the 46 percent that cannot go a month without a paycheque, or the 28 percent who can stretch savings only up to four months, losing their jobs, falling into arrears, and being evicted is more likely an everyday concern.

––––––––––––

Wages are too low. Rents are too high. And the notion that something is out of order with the rental market and that some genius technical solution can fix the problem is, at best, deceptive. Markets are doing what markets do: trans-ferring income from workers to the capital-owning class. As far as the landlord class is concerned, the rental housing market is working just fine.

CHAPTER TWO

Myths about the Tenant Class

~~There is nothing wrong with owning or wanting to own a home, if that's your thing. It only becomes a problem when society ascribes certain qualities to people who own while holding unflattering views about those who don't. That's the case in Canada, where homeownership is the hallmark of a successful middle-class life, and renting is perceived as a temporary state in one's life, a stepping stone to something better. Renting past early adulthood feels like falling behind, failing.~~ A recent Ipsos survey found that 55 percent of Canadians aged 18 to 34 "won't feel that they have accomplished what they need to in their life until they own their own home."[1] The media feeds this fear with story after story on the increasingly difficult access to homeownership, which some journalists call the "Canadian dream."[2] Politicians know these statistics and act accordingly.

In the 2021 federal election, Prime Minister Justin Trudeau presented his housing platform to the country with a tweet stating, "we have a plan to support the next generation of homeowners."[3] Most of the plan refers to renters as aspiring homebuyers, with fewer references for tenants living in poverty. At least two-thirds of tenants don't fall in either category,[4] but they were not mentioned. One of the proposals in the plan was a tax-free saving account to help first-time homebuyers with down payments, for which only Canadians under 40 years of age would be eligible. The message was clear: the government will help young people to buy a house up to a certain age; after that, slackers are on their own.

Many of these government programs simply help first-time homebuyers to take on debt larger than they should. By injecting additional cash into the housing market, these programs may push house prices up, making the problem worse. It doesn't matter. Middle-class families sign up for them, take on financially unsound mortgages and indebt themselves to historically high levels. Some pay thousands and thousands of dollars more than the asking price for a home. And it is not uncommon to forgo home inspections on houses that, if everything goes well, will consume most of their disposable income for years. It's unbelievable. News stories and data analysis describe this irrational behaviour as people doing what it takes to achieve the ownership dream.[5] The question that is less-often asked is, how much do you have to hate being a tenant to make these absurd purchases? How much of it relates to wanting to own property versus feeling pressure to escape the social status of tenants?

It takes a different kind of study to look into buyers' motivation at the individual level. For our purposes here, the point is that repeatedly portraying renting as an undesirable situation, an incomplete life project—in short as failure—renders "tenant" a lesser status than "homeowner." Negative views about renting harm the sense of worth of people in the 33 percent of Canadian households that rent,[6] and they have negative political implications. Constant exposure to negative views about one's class makes organizing efforts more difficult.

Early class analyses focused on economic processes and the material conditions necessary for a revolution. With time, Marxists started wondering why the Russian Revolution of 1917 had not spread to other countries. German social theorists at the Frankfurt School were among the first to take a stab at answering the question, starting in the 1920s, though the Institute later turned focus to broader and more philosophical questions. Antonio Gramsci spent his time in Italian prisons (1929 to 1935) trying to understand why workers embrace the cultural habits and worldview of the dominant class. In the 1940s, Brazilian adult educator Paulo Freire began to develop pedagogies focused on teaching workers to understand the world through their own experience rather than through the eyes of elites.

These theoretical streams—among others—produced nuanced analyses of how mass media, popular culture, and everyday language exalt certain ideals and population groups while belittling the life experience of other groups and misrecognizing their identities. Much of this research became utterly academic, but their original political motivation of transforming capitalist societies makes some of the insights still useful to class-based social movements.

Freire, for instance, insisted that militants interested in understanding the world in order to transform it must grapple with the subjective and objective reality of oppressed classes. Material exploitation happens within cultural contexts full of symbols and meanings that shape the perceived order of things. For Freire, analyses of subjectivities that do not directly inform political action are useless. By the same token, political action that fails to understand the subjective aspects of oppression cannot be successful.[7]

In a similar line of argument, American political philosopher Nancy Fraser uses the terms redistribution and recognition to describe the two broad types of claims made by social movements. Social groups subject to economic injustice demand policies that redistribute income and wealth. Social groups who are not valued or outright despised by the dominant culture fight to have their identities recognized as of equal worth to others. Fraser contends that most real-world examples of social injustice include both economic injustice and misrecognition, with one type of injustice at times more prominent than the other. Social movements decide how to weigh those two types of demands.[8]

Tenants face both forms of injustice: landlords extract ever more profits for the tenant class, while Canadian society treats tenants as an inferior, less accomplished bunch. Cultural practices and symbols praise homeownership and sideline people who rent past a certain age. The assumption is that they haven't pulled themselves up by their own bootstraps or they would own a home. Addressing this misrecognition of tenants is also an important aspect of the struggle for housing justice.

There are at least four widespread myths that can have a damaging effect on organizing efforts. They are: renting is a phase people grow out of, tenants don't pay property taxes, a large share of tenants don't work, and everyone would do anything to own a home. Spoiler alert: they are all inaccurate, prejudicial views.

RENTING IS NOT A PHASE

A common strategy for sweeping economic injustice under the carpet is to depict it as something that happens to the youth, who will eventually be fine. For instance, conservative economists repeatedly present minimum-wage earners as youth living with their parents who will one day earn grown-up wages.[9] This is not the full picture. Minimum-wage earners comprise other population groups, including a disproportional share of senior workers.[10]

Similarly, tenants are often depicted as university students living in precarious housing, almost as a rite of passage to adulthood, collecting funny stories to tell their children later in life. Or in the many news stories about soaring housing prices, as young couples struggling to build financial security. Yes, those people are a portion of the tenant population, but not all of it. While, on average, tenants are a bit younger than homeowners, 70 percent of primary maintainers in tenant households are older than 35, and 22 percent are older than 65.[11] If there is a stereotypical tenant, that person recalls using a fax machine.

Most of these tenants are either not interested in buying a home or can't afford to do so. In a 2021 Angus Reid Institute survey, 21 percent of tenants declared they are "not interested in buying a home"; another 45 percent affirmed they "would like to buy a home now, but can't afford it"; and 25 percent stated they "do not ever expect to be able to afford to buy a home." Two percent expected to inherit a home someday, and only the remaining 7 percent were "in the market now, looking to purchase a home."[12] In other words, 93 percent of renters who responded to the survey will not stop renting any time soon. Phrases like "the next generation of homeowners," "millennials can't afford homes after exiting the basement,"[13] and "Canadian dream slipping out of reach"[14] are both inaccurate and misleading. They suggest that an entire generation was in the succession line for a home, and that has been pulled out of their hands.

That was never the case, especially for racialized population groups. Homeownership rates have fluctuated between 60 percent and 69 percent in the past 50 years (1971 to 2021), meaning that on any given day, between 30 and 40 percent of the population did not own a home.[15] The rates are lower for most racialized groups, except for the Chinese and South Asian communities. Ownership rates for people who identify as Black (45 percent), Arab (47 percent), Indigenous (50 percent), or Latin American (51 percent) are significantly lower than for people who identity as white (76 percent). And while the rate increased for white people between 2006 and 2016, it dropped for Black people.[16]

Maybe a (disproportionally white) share of the population who grew up in an owned home expected to own one, too. Without belittling the disappointment of these folks, the big (and more accurate) picture is that the housing market always excluded a large chunk of the population, for whom homeownership was not impossible but never at reach either. Their parents rent, and they will likely rent for years to come. For them, renting is not a phase.

TENANTS PAY PROPERTY TAXES

Municipal property taxes pay, in full or in part, for many public services that directly impact people's lives, including water, sewage, snow removal, garbage collection, recreation services, public transit, park maintenance, road maintenance, schools (partially), some long-term care homes, social housing (in some provinces), and libraries. All city residents have the right to call for more or better or different services, organize like-minded neighbours, and try to effect change. In practice, this sense of entitlement is more common among homeowners, because they pay their taxes directly to governments.

In the case of tenants, property taxes are included in their rent and may not be perceived as a contribution to city services and programs. As the Federation of Rental-housing Providers of Ontario (a landlord association) explained in a 2015 document, "Most tenants do not know this, but on average, they are paying an incredible $190 per month in property tax." The document refers to multi-residential properties, mostly apartment buildings and rental row houses, but tenants in other types of units also pay property taxes. Private landlords who rent single-family houses, condos, rooms, and basements pay property taxes and treat it as an operating cost. As with any business, the price of the product covers all costs, plus a margin of profit. Landlords pass the cost of property taxes on to tenants, the same as taxi companies pass gas taxes to their riders. The Federation document concluded, "It's included (and hidden) in their rent. But they are paying it."[17]

The way information on municipal budgets is presented by governments and discussed in the media is part of the reason why tenants are not seen as property taxpayers. Take the City of Toronto, for example. Its budget process is transparent compared to other governments in the country and closely covered by the media. Every year, city staff release charts of "Where the Money Comes From," showing that about one-third of the city's revenues come from "Property Taxes." Anyone who stumbles into the 2020 budget documents quickly learns that 33 percent of the revenue for that year, or $4.3 billion, came from property taxes. Fewer people will know that there are four types of property taxes: residential, multi-residential (rental units), commercial, and industrial. Anyone interested in learning the share of property taxes paid by tenants in multi-residential buildings (not including those in the secondary market) has to dig deep into the 747-page budget document and do some calculations.[18] (Which I did;

the answer was close to half a billion dollars in property
taxes in 2020.)

Not surprisingly, given how the information is presented, property tax debates focus on homeowners.
Toronto Star columnist Matt Elliott once wrote a column
arguing that increasing property taxes was the best option
for Toronto. His main argument: Toronto homeowners pay
lower property taxes than homeowners in other Greater
Toronto Area (GTA) cities.[19] His charts clearly showed
the gap. It was a progressive and incisive argument, like
many others he has put forward over the years. Yet, the
continued focus on homeowners inadvertently reinforces
the idea that tenants do not pay these taxes.

This is an example of how the tenant class is regularly
mischaracterized—even by progressive voices—in subtle
ways that contribute to misrecognition. These subtle-
ties matter a great deal. Conservative homeowners have
repeatedly used "taxpayer" or "ratepayer" as a badge of
honour and way of sidelining other voices in their neighbourhoods.[20] The tenant struggle for recognition includes
challenging these false claims.

TENANTS WORK SAME AS HOMEOWNERS

Most tenants work. This is an obvious statement to anyone who ever stood at a bus stop by a high-rise apartment
building. Yet, part of the stigma against tenants derives
from a common North American myth: anyone who works
hard can pull themselves up by their bootstraps. Since it is
assumed that everyone wants to own a home, those who
don't must not be working hard enough. But that's not true.

The statistics for tenants and homeowners are virtually
the same, within a couple of percentage points. According
to the Census data (2016), among the population 15 years
of age and older, 64 percent of those living in a rented

home were active in the labour force, compared to 66 percent of those living in a home owned by a family member.[21] According to Canadian Income Survey data (2017), 21 percent of tenants and 19 percent of homeowners did not work in the surveyed year. According to tax filer data (2018), the employment rate for Torontonians was 70 percent for those who did not own property and 72 percent for those who did. In Vancouver, employment was higher for those who did not own property (77 percent) than for those who did (70 percent).[22]

The Canadian Housing Survey (2018) also asked respondents for their main activity in the past 12 months. Again, there were striking similarities. Among tenants in private rental units, 55 percent said "work" (compared to 55 percent of homeowners), 3.7 percent said "caring for other family members" (compared to 3.6 percent of owners), and 0.8 percent said "doing volunteer work" (compared to 0.7 percent of owners). A lower share of renters in social or affordable housing (24 percent) listed work as their main activity. They were also much more likely to live with a long-term illness or disability (three times more likely than other renters and six times more likely than homeowners). Renters in social and affordable housing did twice as much volunteer (2.1 percent) and caring work (6.9 percent) than other folks. They were also more likely to have spent most of the year looking for work (three times more likely than homeowners).[23] In summary, according to multiple data sources, tenants work at very similar rates to homeowners.

But they are paid less. The lowest-paid occupations in Canada, measured in total annual employment income, include service support, sales support, service supervisors, service representatives, professional and technical occupations in arts and culture, construction labourers, manufacturing processing, and paraprofessional community and education services. At the top of the pay scale, we find senior and middle management occupations and professionals in various fields. Comparing the share of tenants in each of these occupations with the percentage of the total population who hold these jobs, there is a negative correlation (R^2 = 0.73) between the tenant share ratio and wages.[24] In other words, the lower the wages, the more likely tenants will be overrepresented.

The misconception that tenants work less is partly fuelled by the fact that close to a third of tenant households receive government transfers.[25] This figure is regularly mentioned in housing debates. In my experience, more often than not, the person citing the statistics is advocating for adequate social assistance rates—which is yet another example of a progressive argument that inadvertently reinforces negative views about the tenant class.

Government transfers are the major source of income for 16 percent of homeowners—a less-often cited figure.[26] Since a disproportional 46 percent of tenant households are persons living alone (compared to 22 percent of homeowners), using the household as the unit of analysis overstates the point.[27] In most datasets, government transfers include employment insurance (E.I.) and workers who did not qualify for E.I. due to its strict rules and applied for social assistance instead. The category also includes contributory public pension plans. Finally, if transfers are a source, or even the major source of income, it doesn't mean people don't work, only that wages are a smaller share of their income. People in receipt of income supports work when they can and to the extent of their ability. They also take care of family members and volunteer in their communities.

It shouldn't matter whether people—tenants and

homeowners alike—earn wages, receive income supports, or both. Everyone relies on a combination of sources of income, public services, and public infrastructure, depending on various factors, including age. The reason for making this distinction here is that emphasis on government transfers serves to explain high rents away—as the fault of governments who don't raise assistance rates—and to negatively depict tenants as people who don't work hard enough. That's false.

NOT EVERY TENANT IS A WANNABE HOMEOWNER

Infatuated with homeownership, the social status and the prospects of wealth it brings, Canadians pay little attention to the benefits of renting, of which there are many. In "Renter, here are seven financial advantages over home-owners," an unusual title for a *Globe and Mail* personal finance column, Rob Carrick lists some of these advantages. Most are related to savings on insurance, maintenance, property taxes (partially), and car ownership costs (possibly). Carrick also lists labour-force mobility, the ability to follow a career opportunity wherever it takes you, which is more complicated and costs more for homeowners than renters.[28] To this list, we could add that people with less debt can devote more time to activities unrelated to paying and maintaining a financial asset, be it a hobby, a second occupation, or a political cause.

The neighbours across the street from me are a great example of this. Ayse and André live in Manor Park Estates, a row housing complex built in the 1950s on the east side of Ottawa. Ayse migrated to Canada in her 20s, worked as a travel agent for more than a decade, stayed home until the children started grade school, then returned to the labour market. Extremely energetic, she says things like, "I just have to change my winter tires first; it won't take me long." André grew up in mining towns across Ontario. After receiving a college and a bachelor's degree in engineering sciences, he worked his way up in construction, from crew leader to site supervisor to project manager. His son once told me, "Go get my dad, he can fix this, he can fix anything." The boy was right. With their combined income, energy, and skills, they could buy a house and rebuild it inside out. They prefer to rent instead.

It shouldn't need an explanation, but they are often asked for one. I heard it a few times. ~~In short, buying a home would drain all their disposable income and time. They have other life projects to which they would rather devote money and time, including the kids, volunteer work, and outdoor activities in the Ottawa-Gatineau region.~~ André considers starting a small business, which would take a chunky bite into their savings. Ayse likes the city, but as an immigrant, she knows sometimes you have to pick up and move. Many people associate homeownership with financial security, but Ayse values mobility. "As long as we can go where the work takes us, we'll be fine, the kids will be fine," she told me.[29]

Manor Park Estates is what housing experts call "naturally occurring affordable housing," rent-controlled units that haven't been gentrified, where rents are below average market prices without government subsidies. In 2021, a vacant two-bedroom, two-level row house in Manor Park Estates rented for $1,250, heating and parking included. Due to rent controls, families in units they had been occupying for some time paid less; one long-term tenant paid $1,087.[30] In the same year, the average rent for similar-size units in Ottawa (not including condos) was $1,840.[31] The difference between average rents and rents in Manor Park Estates allows families to live better, afford some of the activities they enjoy, and maybe put some money away.

Ayse and André are amazing parents, active community members, and awesome neighbours. They have a great social life and exciting plans for the future. This may not be the "Canadian dream" that some media and politicians tout, but that doesn't bother them.

The owner of Manor Park Estates has an ambitious redevelopment plan in motion, which will densify the area over the next 25 years and likely reposition the row houses as higher-end units. He has signed a memorandum of understanding committing to offer every tenant a similar or better unit, grandfather rent controls, and cover all moving expenses to the new units.[32] Ayse and André appreciate the commitment but want to ensure other tenants know about it. They joined a working group created by Manor Park's neighbourhood association, then quit it. Meeting after meeting, homeowners discussed strategies to oppose densification, making little space for the two tenants in the room to express concerns about what will happen to *their* homes. At the time of writing, they are involved in a community-benefits agreement working group led by the municipal councillor's office. They are having amicable discussions with the landlord about making a larger share of the new units truly affordable for working-class families like themselves. And they are starting to organize the Manor Park Tenant Union.[33]

Renting has many financial and non-financial advantages over ownership. But in addition to the cultural stigma attached to tenants, the dominance of private rentals and profit-seeking landlords prevents a fair comparison between the two. When given a choice between owning and driving a car or relying on an underfunded, unreliable public transit system, many will opt for the car. But would they still choose to drive if cheap and reliable transit was available to them?[34] Similarly, remove the capital-owing class and its

profit motives from rental housing, and it becomes a much
more appealing choice than what it is made out to be.

In addition to economic injustice, tenants face stigma. In a
society where homeownership is the hallmark of a successful middle-class life, renting is equated with broken dreams,
falling behind, not making it. Tenants are second rate.
Unfounded misconceptions about tenants are reinforced
in everyday conversation, policy debates, the media, and
the way Canadian history is told. Even advocates pushing
for progressive policies sometimes inadvertently propagate
negative views of the tenant class.

In addition to class-based prejudice, some tenants face
other forms of discrimination. In particular, tenants who
are racialized, immigrants, Indigenous, women, gender
non-conforming, and living with disabilities experience
economic injustice and misrecognition in compounded
ways.[35] Many power dynamics and forms of discrimination shape tenant-landlord relations. The focus on social
class is not intended to undermine the importance of
these other struggles but to emphasize that which all tenants have in common: a landlord that extracts profit from
a basic human necessity, shelter. Landlords are not only
allowed to enrich at the cost of people who need a roof,
but are often praised for it. That's partly because society
holds unflattering views of tenants, and partly because of
widespread misconceptions about the landlord class.

CHAPTER THREE

But What about the Landlords?

At the onset of the COVID-19 pandemic, before the Canadian Emergency Relief Benefit (CERB) launch, the Canadian Centre for Policy Alternatives (CCPA) published a report showing that nearly half of tenant households relying on employment income had only up to one month's worth of income in savings.[1] The report argued that these households would not be able to weather the economic hardships of lockdown measures. With historically high unemployment rates and no indication of when the economy would reopen, thousands of tenant families risked eviction during a global health crisis. Following the report's release, I filled numerous media requests where I argued that Canada needed a national rent forgiveness program.[2] A common reaction to that argument was, "But what about the landlords?"

The reason why the well-being of landlords is equated with that of tenant families—even during a pandemic—is that landlords are seen as individuals, families, and "mom and pop" shops whose financial security depends on their rental income. The widespread notion of "struggling landlords" is a grave mischaracterization of the rental market. In fact, Canada's landlord class comprises wealthy families, small businesses, corporations, and financial investors. Rent revenue increases their wealth and political influence, allowing them to extract more income from more tenants, amass more wealth, and do it again.

With no single data source on rental property owner-ship, it is difficult to get a precise picture of the compos-ition of Canadian landlords. Datasets with complementary information overlap in confusing ways while containing significant gaps.[3] Many units are rented informally, mak-ing them difficult to catalogue. The market is also con-stantly changing, with thousands of units added to and removed from the housing stock annually. These limita-tions notwithstanding, it is possible to categorize landlords into distinct groups and to estimate the share of the mar-ket each group represents: roughly 12 percent of tenants live in non-market housing; about 38 percent rent from private landlords, mostly wealthy individuals and fam-ilies who own more than one home and a smaller share of homeowners who rent a portion of the home in which they live; approximately 22 percent rent from small busi-nesses; another 20 percent from corporate landlords; and 8 percent live in units owned by financial landlords. These rough estimates provide a good general portrait.

NON-MARKET HOUSING

Rental housing does not have to generate profit. Across the world, several housing models remove profit from the provision of rental units, making them accessible to more people at fairer prices. There are many, often overlapping, names to describe this type of housing; depending on the context, they may mean somewhat different things. Public housing usually refers to units owned by a government agency; non-profit housing is commonly used to designate housing owned and managed by community organizations and other housing providers, not run as a private business;

co-operatives are a form of non-profit housing involving some form of collective ownership and management.

Internationally, the Organisation for Economic Co-operation and Development (OECD) uses "social rental housing" to refer to "residential rental accommodation provided at submarket prices and allocated according to specific rules rather than market mechanisms."[4] In Canada, "social housing" is an umbrella term for all of the above, though it is gradually being replaced by "affordable housing" in public debate. Notably, in the 2021 federal election, the three major federal parties promised to build "affordable housing," avoiding the term "social housing" and blurring the important distinction between privately-owned and non-market rental units. In this book, "non-market housing" refers to the share of the rental housing stock not owned by profit-seeking landlords.

In 2021, 12 percent of all tenants rented from governments, non-profit housing providers, or co-operatives. This figure accounts for approximately 601,000 households, or 4 percent of all households in the country.[5] OECD data provides a lower estimate: about 3.5 percent of households in 2020.[6] Both estimates are below the 7 percent OECD international average. Canada is light years behind the countries at the top of the OECD list (the Netherlands, 34 percent; Austria, 24 percent; and Denmark, 21 percent); it is also far below countries to which it is often compared, namely the United Kingdom (17 percent) and France (14 percent). The United States and Australia have similar averages to Canada, at 3.6 percent and 4.4 percent, respectively.[7]

If Canada is at the bottom of the list today, it was a model to other countries only a few decades ago. According to housing policy expert Greg Suttor, in the 1960s and

1970s Canada's enabling policies and high investment levels in social housing were well regarded internationally.
He calls the period between 1965 and 1973 the "heyday
of social housing." During that period, 10 percent of
newly built rental housing was non-market housing. Deep
poverty would have increased at a much higher rate in
Canada's rapidly growing cities if not for the high number of new social housing units. Canada continued to build
large but decreasing numbers of social housing until the
early 1990s. Since then, the country went back to a model
wherein social housing is provided only to a small number
of very low-income families, and the private sector provides almost all other housing.[8]

Tenants in non-market rental housing pay significantly
less for rent. In 2018, tenants in government-owned housing paid, on average, $460 for a one-bedroom apartment,
those in co-operative and non-profit housing paid $630,
whereas tenants renting from a private company or individual paid $970. For two-bedroom units, the respective
values were $700, $840, and $1,130. For three-bedroom
units, the values were $850, $870, and $1,350.[9] To state
the obvious, when we remove profit from rental housing,
rents drop, by a lot.

But is non-market housing a good place to live, raise a
family, or move for retirement? This is ultimately a question for people who live or have lived in non-market and
public-owned housing. However, the data suggests that
non-market housing does not stand out as significantly
different in shape, quality, and level of tenant satisfaction
from private market rentals.

The stereotypical complex of dense social housing
buildings that may be familiar from US television portray-
als is more common in the United States than in Canada,
where the height of social housing production coincided

with a private rental construction boom. According to Suttor, in the 1960s and 1970s public housing units were often integrated with private rental construction and scattered across cities, especially the growing suburbs of Toronto, Montreal, and Vancouver. The outcome was a mix of public and private rentals, more low-rise buildings, and more row houses than this common stereotype.[10]

According to Canadian Housing Survey data, public housing is only slightly behind market rentals when it comes to the state of repairs. In 2018, it shows 8 percent of tenants living in private rentals, 9 percent in co-operative and non-profit housing, and 11 percent in government-owned housing assessed that their units needed major repairs. The share of tenants who assessed their units as safe and secure was also similar for those living in non-profit housing (52 percent), private rentals (53 percent), and government-owned housing (54 percent). It is a sad statement that only about half of all tenants feel safe at home, but living in non-market housing is not a statistically relevant factor.[11]

However, government housing has not been built in large volumes in Canada for decades, and those units are getting old compared to private units. Funding is a problem. In the 1990s, the federal government passed the responsibility for social housing on to provinces, some of which passed the buck further down to municipal governments, who often did not invest enough in upkeep. As a result, many public housing agencies have acquired a bad reputation.[12] These claims are not baseless. In 2016, the Toronto Community Housing Corporation (TCHC) had 400 units assessed as beyond repair. In 2019, the TCHC found demolishing and rebuilding units easier than renovating them.[13] For many years, tenants lived in crumbling, hazardous, and undignified TCHC units before they were shut down. Not that the private rental market is necessarily any better. Data shows a similar share of private rental units in a deplorable state of repair.

The hallmark of non-market housing is that rents are lower—because profit is not part of the equation. That is a big deal. Non-market housing also provides tenants more stability, as rent increases more slowly and evictions are less common. But, in addition to being priced fairly, housing needs to be decent and well maintained. In this respect, non-market housing offers no guarantees. Non-market landlords can be and, in many instances, have been terrible landlords. In those cases, tenants have no choice but to organize and confront landlords, same as they do with other types of landlords.

Non-market housing, for all its advantages, is notoriously difficult to get into. In 2018, 283,800 Canadian households (2 percent of all households in the country) had at least one family member on a waiting list for non-market housing. Statistics Canada reports that "of these households, almost two-thirds (61 percent) or 172,800 households were on a waiting list for two years or longer."[14] "Longer" being the operative word. A closer look shows that one in four has been waiting for eight years or more.[15] In the meantime, they rent in the private, for-profit market, along with most Canadian tenants.

PRIVATE LANDLORDS

With only 12 percent of tenants living in non-market housing, the majority rent market units. But market units don't always mean tall apartment buildings. In fact, 38 percent of tenants rent homes not specifically built for renting but that serve that purpose, including detached single-family houses, semi-detached houses, townhouses, condos, duplex and triplex apartments, basement units, and other types of secondary units. The technical term for this portion of the rental market is "secondary rental market"; combined with non-market housing, it comprises roughly half of rental units in the country.[16] There is no standard name for for-profit landlords in the secondary rental market. For simplicity, we will call them private landlords.

The media commonly portrays landlords as families whose financial security is on par with their tenants. Since, in many cases, rental income complements earnings from employment, pensions, investments, and other sources, it is perceived as money that families depend on to get by. This view misses that private landlords use the rental market to amass wealth. They charge tenants more than it costs to maintain a rental unit and keep the profit for themselves. A family that pays the mortgage on a second home with the rent collected on it ends up with two homes. This is not only legal but something that is praised in Canadian culture. People who put a down payment on a second home, only to rent it and have tenants cover their mortgage costs, are seen as astute and entrepreneurial.

The problem is that entrepreneurial, profit-making, wealth-growing investments must be accurately portrayed. A family that owns multiple homes is wealthy; it is not scraping to get by. In 2019, the average net worth of multiple-property-owner families in Canada was $1.7 million (excluding mortgage debt).[17] Private landlords may not be multi-billion-dollar corporations but they are not scraping to get by either; they are high-income households, many of whom live in expensive detached houses while collecting rent from other properties.[18]

Going back to the question the media frequently asks me (But what about the landlords?), the simple answer is, they will be fine! In contrast, tenants who miss rent have already skipped meals, sent kids to school with inadequate winterwear, walked miles in the cold to save transit fares, and sacrificed other basic needs in trying to pay rent because the risk of being evicted is terrifying. Tenants don't choose to fall into arrears. The housing security of private landlords should not be equated to that of financially insecure tenant families. One is accumulating wealth and has two or more homes to choose from; the other is at the risk of becoming homeless.

Amid the COVID-19 pandemic, the *Toronto Star* ran a story on the negative impacts of Ontario's Landlord and Tenant Board closure titled, "Pandemic creating a 'nightmare' for local landlords and tenants."[19] Here is an excerpt from that story:

> While many tenants have been waiting to get hearing dates before the Landlord and Tenant Board to resolve their housing issues, landlords have also started speaking out about not being able to pay their bills due to delinquent tenants. There is a concern that given the lingering frustration of lost income and mounting unresolved issues—many delayed now for a year or more—some landlords are giving up and selling their property. . . . "We are small-time landlords, this was our first investment property, ever," said the daughter of the couple who purchased [one such] house. "It ended up being way more of a nightmare than anything."[20]

The story repeatedly depicts "small-time landlords" as families and selling the investment property as a great loss.

Let's look at that story from another angle: a private investor looked for a low-risk investment with high returns and opted to inject money into Canada's real estate market. The pandemic negatively impacted operations and the investor opted to shift to a different portfolio. Since housing prices rise fast, the investor realized gains at the sale of the asset despite some operational losses.

The "small-time landlord" made money in the flipping of the house, even if the plan to get tenants to pay for their second house fell through. There is nothing legally wrong with the investment, and many people find it morally acceptable or even commendable. But it ought to be treated for what it is: an investor seeking to make a high profit, not the story of a struggling family.

———————

There is a small group of private landlords that do fit the "small-time landlord" description. These are single-property owners who rent a portion of the homes in which they live. It is reasonable to assume this group relies on rent to cover their essential living costs; otherwise, they would live in the entire home themselves. Examples include a senior on a fixed income who rents a room to a student, or someone who works in a low-wage industry (artists for example) and rents the second room in a condo to make up for low earnings in their field. These cases exist, but they are a small fraction of homeowners.[21] Popular culture and the media greatly exaggerate the share of landlords in this "struggling-to-pay-their-own-mortgage" category, which helps to build a positive image of the real estate industry.

In addition to these romanticized descriptions of private landlords in mainstream media, personal experiences may also blur the important distinction between individual landlords and the class to which they belong. It happened to me. Right after my first child was born, my spouse and I rented the second floor of a house in Toronto. In inquiring about the unit, I learned that the landlord, Said, lived on the main floor of the house. Right away, I asked whether a newborn baby would be a problem. He sounded offended when he answered, "babies are a part of life, and they would never be a problem." We took the place. Every morning Said and his girlfriend pretended they had not heard the baby crying during the night. Storage space was not included in the rent, but after realizing how tight the unit was for a family, Said began sharing his garage with us. He was a decent, thoughtful man who belonged to the small "struggling-to-pay-their-own-mortgage" category.

But then there was John, the landlord of a basement apartment we'd rented a few years earlier. The crumbling kitchen ceiling was never fixed, he did not allow us to cook certain types of food because the smells bothered him, and he eventually imposed a rule that we could not cook after 8:00 p.m. despite us both working late. John was also a "small-time landlord," but a jerk nevertheless.

Said and John were very different people who had one thing in common: they belonged to the class that owned rental property, whereas my spouse and I belonged to the class that paid rent. Personal relationships should never be assumed to protect people in a disadvantaged power position. This notion has been highly criticized, especially by gender analyses showing the senseless amount of exploitation and abuse within households and in other settings, where knowing someone well offers no protection whatsoever.

Democracies are rule-based societies where the laws apply to everyone, procedures exist for people to claim rights, and people can express their views freely. The opposite of democracy is not only authoritarianism but also patrimonialism, which refers to political contexts in which a person (usually a man) can ignore laws and procedures, and treat everything as belonging to him and everyone as depending on his favour. In a democratic society like Canada, tenants should not be at the whim of landlords, worried about being on their right side and avoiding doing things that could upset them, even if that is simply cooking dinner after getting home late from work.

In Canada, laws, tenancy acts, and provincial documents are meant to protect tenants. However, there is the law, and then there is practice. The day-to-day interactions with private landlords often occur outside formal channels and ultimately come down to power relationships between the two sides. Lucky tenants with decent landlords may not have any problems other than paying high rents. Other tenants may be at the mercy of a John—or someone worse. The well-being of a third of Canadian households cannot be left to luck.

While half of tenants rent from non-market providers and private landlords, the other half lives in purpose-built rental housing: units built specifically for the private rental market. Most purpose-built units (96 percent) are apartment buildings, with row housing making up the rest.[22] They are owned by small businesses, large corporations, and financial landlords. The next sections look at each in turn.

SMALL BUSINESSES

Small businesses own roughly 22 percent of rental units in the country.[23] They are often called "mom and pop" landlords, a positive, almost endearing characterization that reinforces the idea that these landlords are struggling families. In urban centres, apartment buildings owned by this type of landlord have 44 units, on average; in Toronto the average is 151 units.[24] Even if a landlord owns a single, average-size building in Vancouver, that business's gross annual revenue in 2021 was close to $800,000. In Toronto, "mom and pop" landlords collected nearly $3 million in rent for each average-size building. (Mom must have a large purse!)[25]

These businesses also hold assets worth millions and millions of dollars, which increase in value fast. This is not to say these business owners don't carry debt, incur depreciation costs, have unexpected revenue losses and cost increases, and sometimes go into the red. The point is simply they are not families, they are businesses, and should be discussed as such.

Overall, small businesses charge less for similar-size units than corporate landlords, at least in part because they own older buildings. But in the hot markets of large urban centres, they push rents nearly as high as corporate landlords. In 2016, small businesses in Vancouver charged only 3 percent less than corporate landlords charged for two-bedroom units; it was 2 percent less in Toronto. As with the case of private landlords, the size of the "mom and pop" landlord does not fundamentally alter power dynamics. They own rental property, dictate how much workers can keep of their earnings, and may try to evict families if there is money to be made.

An ethnographic study of rental housing in the American city of Milwaukee richly depicts these asymmetrical power relations and the ruthlessness of some of the so-called mom and pop landlords.[26] The study shows that when these small businesses operate with thin profit margins, they will cut costs wherever they can, neglecting properties, ignoring health and safety guidelines, disregarding tenant rights, and pushing tenants out whenever opportunities for gains present themselves. If they are desperate, they will do whatever it takes to stay in business. Are they struggling "mom and pop" landlords or simply "slumlords"?

It depends on who you ask. Small businesses are often

portrayed as people who know their customers and employ-
ees well, spend time with them, and have their interests at
heart. Sometimes this argument goes further by presenting
the interests of both classes as the same. We see this every
time a provincial government announces a minimum-wage
increase, and right-wing think tanks contend that the measure "will likely kill thousands of jobs and hurt those it is
intended to help."[27] Small business owners are always the
face of anti-minimum-wage increase campaigns; workers
are encouraged to side with their bosses and choose job
security over a raise. The survival of the business is in the
employee's best interest, the argument goes.

A similar argument in rental housing is that "small-
time landlords" may sell the property to a heartless corporation if the business does not continue to make a profit, so
tenants should accept rent increases and not demand too
many expensive repairs. Workers and tenants who are nice
get to keep what they have, maybe eventually have a repair
or two done, whereas things may get worse for those who
choose not to co-operate.

This is fearmongering. If a small business cannot pay
workers a minimum wage, what is the point of continuing
that business? Shut the doors. The same goes for landlords
that cannot keep properties well maintained; we are better
off without them. Governments should purchase, repair,
and transfer those units to the non-market stock.

CORPORATIONS

In turn, corporate landlords are irrefutably large and profitable firms. Some hold hundreds of buildings and tens of
thousands of apartments. They own an estimated 20 percent of all rental units in Canada. More economically and
politically powerful than private landlords and small businesses, but subject to less transparency requirements than

financial landlords, corporations are tough adversaries for
tenant movements. And they are growing fast.

Homestead Land Holdings, one of the largest landlords
in the country, owns 225 buildings and more than 27,000
units. Some corporations manage units for other real estate
investors in addition to their own. Minto Properties, for
example, owns 299 buildings and manages an additional
21 for investors. Other corporations specialize in managing
properties. That is the case of Sterling Karamar Property
Management; they serve as landlords for hire in 134 buildings across Ontario.

In the capitalist logic of profit and accumulation, the
bigger a corporation, the bigger it grows over time, through
new acquisitions and mergers. Take Hazelview Investments
(formerly Timbercreek), for example. Its portfolio grew
from 16,055 to 21,580 units between 2015 and 2020, a
34 percent increase in only five years.[28] Starlight Investments
bought 500 units in Victoria in a single acquisition during
the COVID-19 pandemic.[29] That's how they roll.

For tenant movements, corporate landlords present
opportunities and challenges. On the one hand, the sheer
size of these corporations precludes any attempt to depict
them as struggling families or "mom and pop" shops. The
media usually calls them "one of the largest landlords in
Canada," "real estate giant," and other similar terms, helping to sway public opinion in favour of the tenant families
they might be trying to crush. On the other hand, corporations have more resources to deploy against tenants.

In 2019, Hazelview demolished 150 townhouses in
Heron Gate, Ottawa, forcing more than 500 people from
their homes. The evicted tenants, 90 percent of whom were
immigrants and racialized residents, launched a human
rights complaint against the City of Ottawa and the corporate landlord.[30] It has taken a great amount of courage,

organization, and resource-pooling on the part of the Herongate Tenant Coalition to take a corporation with an endless amount of resources to court.[31]

Alexander Ferrer, a Los Angeles-based tenant advocate, explains that large real estate investors can use many legal and accounting tricks to avoid liability and accountability. A common strategy he has seen is for the same investor to hold multiple companies with different names, making them look unrelated from the outside. When disputes with tenants or predatory practices in one property become public, they are not associated with the rest of the portfolio. "To be clear, no tenant advocate will defend the virtue of small landlords, many of whom treat tenants capriciously and employ predatory profit maximization strategies similar to those used by corporate property owners. Yet corporate structures make patterns of abuse harder to root out."[32]

Corporate landlords have professional management, administrative staff, accountants, lawyers, and security personnel working for them around the clock. Tenants are up against platoons of corporate staff, especially when things get ugly. For example, in Ontario, the above-guideline rent increase (AGI) applications allow landlords to circumvent rent controls by arguing they incurred additional maintenance expenses that year. Landlords must gather evidence of those necessary expenses and fill out paperwork to make their case. These applications are not an operational burden for corporations because they are part of someone's job description and pay for themselves. Each AGI approved generates high returns in rent revenue.

On the tenant side, organizing a building against an AGI takes an enormous effort—countless hours of non-paid work in the evenings and weekends. Corporate landlords will deploy lawyers and public relations specialists if the fight gets ugly. In contrast, at best, tenants can count on some support from a legal aid clinic and maybe a sympathetic reporter. This is class warfare at its rawest.

FINANCIAL LANDLORDS

Financial landlords make other landlords look good in comparison. They represent the extreme of capitalism: the world transformed into one big casino, where investors play with people's lives, trying to make big money. With a keyboard stroke, an investor on one side of the globe can sell the homes of hundreds of families, transferring their fates to yet another investor, neither of whom has ever set foot in the neighbourhood where those families live. Every day, thousands of individual investors move money between portfolios according to the latest financial advice. For large, small, corporate, and private investors, these are merely figures moving from one computer screen to another. Yet, somewhere in the world, an eviction notice is printed and slipped under someone's door because of these transactions. The soon-to-be-evicted family was not playing money games but now stands to lose the most.

Unlike other landlords, financial landlords are not in the business of buying, owning, maintaining, and renting units. They do those things, but that is not their primary business. They are financial firms whose core business consists of buying things which they call assets, then partitioning, selling, and trading them. In many instances, financial firms have a formal obligation to maximize returns for their clients; also, the higher the returns, the higher the end-of-year bonuses for the people working at these firms. Real Estate Investment Trusts (REITs) are the largest type of financial landlords. Other types include pension funds, insurance, and asset management companies. Combined, financial landlords own roughly 8 percent of rental units in the country, though that share is growing fast.[33]

Since 1996, financial investors have been acquiring large quantities of rental housing from small businesses and corporate landlords to transform them into financial assets. This is happening across the world as capital knows no borders, and governments have repeatedly failed to regulate financial markets. In a watershed report submitted to the United Nations General Assembly in 2017, Leilani Farha, a Canadian housing advocate who served as the UN Special Rapporteur on adequate housing from 2014 to 2020, sounded the alarm about this unfolding disaster:

> Housing and real estate markets have been transformed by corporate finance, including banks, insurance and pension funds, hedge funds, private equity firms and other kinds of financial intermediaries with massive amounts of capital and excess liquidity. . . . Housing and commercial real estate have become the "commodity of choice" for corporate finance, and the pace at which financial corporations and funds are taking over housing and real estate in many cities is staggering.[34]

Planning scholar Martine August was one of the first researchers to document this trend in Canada, especially the growth and tactics of REITs, and her work continues to be an invaluable source of information on the subject.[35] REITs pool funds from individual and institutional investors by selling shares (called "units") through several financial institutions, including the major banks. Anyone can acquire REIT shares, and in many cases, it is possible to buy and sell them online. REITs manage these rental properties (in most cases), collect rents, pay the operating costs for the building, and share the net revenue with investors (called "unit holders"). REITs provide unit holders with regular payments called "distribution." The REIT owns some of the shares, and keeps a portion of the distribution for itself.

~~Legislation enacted in the 1990s exempts REITs from paying corporate taxes, as long as most rent revenue is distributed to shareholders.~~ Individual investors declare distribution income in their income taxes, mostly under "other income," which is the same category private landlords use to declare rental income. Gains made in buying and selling shares are treated as capital gains, and are taxed at lower rates in Canada. (You read it right: capital gains are taxed at a lower rate than employment income, but that is a topic for another day). When investors hold REIT shares under a Tax-Free Savings Account (TFSA) or a Registered Education Savings Plan (RESP), they do not pay taxes on distributions. When shares are held under a Registered Retirement Savings Plan (RRSP), taxes are deferred until the money is withdrawn.

~~REITs provide middle-class individuals with an easy way to invest in real estate.~~ Put simply, people become landlords without ever having to meet the tenants. A dream come true. ~~For high-income individuals with sizable investment portfolios, who likely already own rental properties, REITs provide an opportunity to diversify investments while ensuring liquidity (ability to quickly cash out).~~ The upshot is more and more people betting and trading on other people's homes.

The yellow brick road is not a secret. In a 2019 article in the digital magazine *Money Sense*, a finance expert laments the work involved in maintaining a rental property. Every few months, she receives requests from tenants that lead to her having to call pest management, service a malfunctioning stove, fix a leaking faucet, or do some other repair. "I'm lucky that the monthly rental income covers maintenance issues like this," but the headache is too much, and "it stands in sharp contrast to my experience investing in [REITs], where I simply purchase shares, take a nap and collect juicy dividends."[36] I could not have worded it better myself. The internet is full of similar stories; they are actually part of the REITs' growth strategy.

Financial operators call their strategies to increase rental revenue "repositioning," which sounds rather benign. August explains that elsewhere these strategies are called "squeezing" and "gentrification-by-upgrading."[37] Squeezing is the pure and simple extraction of more money from the same property. In provinces without rent controls, like Alberta, this is done by pushing rents as high as the market will bear. In Ontario, this can be done through a loophole in rent control legislation that allows landlords to apply for AGIs. In other cases, landlords will charge new or higher fees for existing services or facilities, like laundry and parking. Gentrification-by-upgrading requires a bit more work as it involves pushing tenants out through dirty tactics, giving a face-lift to the unit or the building, and targeting advertisements to higher-income tenants. In the absence of rent controls on vacant units (called "vacancy decontrol"), REITs can charge the next tenant a much higher rent, completing the "repositioning" of the unit. This is all done in broad daylight.

Extracting more income from tenants is the first step of REITs' growth strategy. The next is bragging about it, which is done through the publication of financial reports, the presentation of the annual results in investor meetings, and other material targeted at current and prospective investors. A reason for indignation for some is an attractive opportunity for others. The stellar performance touted in

REITs' promotional materials brings in more money from
investors. REITs use the new capital to buy more properties, then reposition them.

   From 1996 to 2021, REITs alone acquired nearly
200,000 apartment units, roughly 10 percent of the
purpose-built stock.[38] Originally, REITs were more present
in provinces without rent controls, where "repositioning"
units is much easier. They owned around 20 percent of
the purpose-built rental stock in Saskatoon, Edmonton,
Regina, and Calgary, in contrast to less than 5 percent of
rental units in Montreal and Vancouver. In the past few
years, they have made large acquisitions across the country, steadily growing their market share.[39] Canada's largest
residential REIT, CAPREIT, grew its portfolio from 35,454
to 45,129 between 2015 and 2020; in only five years, it
became the new landlord of ten thousand tenant families.[40]
   Invest in a loosely regulated sector, extract excess
profit from working families, accumulate large amounts
of capital—repeat. This is the formula that keeps on giving. And what have governments done? In the 2021 federal
election, the Liberal Party's platform included a promise to
review the tax treatment of REITs and curb excess profit
in housing. At the time of writing, this remains a plan to
plan. At the provincial level, parties have also not made
any substantive effort to stop REITs. Canada's political
class pays much lip service to housing affordability, yet
financial landlords publicly brag about making rental units
unaffordable to working-class families. The response does
not seem to be coming from above, if it ever has.

   REITs receive most of the bad press when it comes to
financial landlords, because they are by far the largest financial landlords, and they are more likely to employ aggressive growth strategies than firms with a longer investment
horizon. But we should not let other investors off the hook.

The involvement of pension funds in the financialization of housing is particularly troubling. In recent years, a larger share of Canadian residents has become invested in the exploitation of tenants, even if unknowingly so.

Canada's rental housing market is doing what rental markets do: extract income from working-class families and transfer it to the capital-owning class. Landlords grow wealthy while tenant families experience financial insecurity, just like greedy bosses enrich on the backs of low-wage workers. The dominant "housing crisis" narrative is part of the problem. It exempts landlords and governments from responsibility by suggesting that excessive rents are a new and unexpected problem that requires complex technical solutions. While the experts look for those solutions, the market continues to do its thing.

The characterization of landlords as struggling families and "mom and pop" shops is also central to this depoliticized view of housing. It helps to advance the idea that solutions need to consider the allegedly fragile financial situation of landlords as much as the well-being of tenants. Designing and implementing these solutions is not easy; it requires time, moderation, and many, many consultations. But the fact is that landlords are businesses. Businesses reduce costs as much as possible while raising prices as high as the market will bear to maximize profit. That is what they do. Tenants are cogs in the rental market money-making machine; if they stop producing cash, they are replaced by new cogs.

Economic exploitation is not the only issue. Various theorists in the Marxist tradition have looked into the cultural aspects of class struggles and warned social movements of the importance of fighting on this front. These insights remain relevant today. In Canada, where home-ownership is the hallmark of a successful middle-class life, tenants are up against many myths and lies, including the notion that tenants are young people waiting to grow up and buy a house, that they don't pay municipal property taxes, and that they work less than other groups. None of this is true. Still, false myths can harm an individual's sense of self-worth and hinder organizing efforts by making people feel uncomfortable or even ashamed of belonging to the tenant class.

But none of this is new. Landlords have dug deep into the pockets of tenants since the colonization of what is now called Canada. Settlers pushed Indigenous Peoples off the land, establishing private poverty, and creating rental markets. Some settlers joined the capital-owning side; others ended up on the tenant side. Tenants have organized and fought back since, and continue to do it today.

CHAPTER FOUR

A History of Struggle

History was my favourite subject in school, likely because I grew up in 1980s Brazil, a world of extremes. The military was all-powerful, then it was gone. The economic mess they created, that stayed. Inflation was well above 100 percent a year, every year. Crime rose as fast as prices. Social movements came out from underground, taking over public squares and local governments.

Sometimes I played soccer with kids who ran barefoot on hot asphalt. Sometimes I played with kids who owned many pairs of shoes. I had one pair, but everyone assumed I had more because of my white skin. Some of my relatives were active in the newly created Workers' Party; others missed the good old days of the military regime. Sunday dinner was cancelled for months at a time. On what seemed like a random afternoon, my first-grade teacher stopped the class to tell us that Brazil was passing a new constitution at that exact moment. We just sat there and watched her cry.

I aced most of my history exams in grade school in what was probably a naive attempt to make sense of all of this. Years later, I found myself conducting archival research on Brazilian social movements. One of their struggle tactics was to construct their own memory. In the 1970s, they created a documentation centre that gathered, archived, and distributed campaign materials, popular education booklets, detailed accounts of political actions, videos, audio recordings, and economic analyses of interest to organizers. The centre served as a channel for movements to communicate with each other without the mediation of the media, academia, or other mainstream organizations. In 2010, the more than 100,000 documents collected in the centre's 40 years were stored in an old building resembling a small auto shop. That year, I visited the centre weekly and spent most of my time unlearning the official history I had memorized for all those school exams. I never trusted textbooks again.

Here in Canada, we also have distinct narratives about the country's colonial legacy and history. Scholars Néstor Medina and Becca Whitla have argued that the widespread notion of "Canada as a benign, welcoming, generous, peacekeeping, multicultural nation" avoids a substantive acknowledgement of its troubling colonial past and ongoing effects.[1] The country's history is commonly told in a way that proudly highlights longstanding bonds with Great Britain and France while concealing Canada's role in the colonial projects those countries spearheaded.

The myth of multiculturalism, "a utopic society and nation, in which the diversity of ethnocultural identities is celebrated,"[2] has been instrumental in helping Canadians to see themselves as Europeans but nicer, preventing much-needed reflection on ongoing forms of racism and colonialism. Canada's supporting role in American imperialism is also hidden from view. The country's peacekeeping image conceals a long history of aiding American economic and military excursions abroad.[3] Much work is underway to decolonize knowledge and language and promote a more accurate and sincere understanding of Canada's colonial legacy.

With regard to social policy, there are distinct historical accounts of the expansion of the country's welfare system.[4] The best-known narrative presents a largely harmonious society led by enlightened politicians and noble public servants. Together, they conceived and gradually expanded the country's physical infrastructure, public services, and social programs from World War II to the mid-1980s. Occasionally, narrowed-minded provincial politicians delayed progress, and loud minorities like Quebec separatists disturbed the peace, but the work moved ahead thanks to a committed political elite and a devoted civil service. This narrative relies heavily on state documents, biographies of eminent politicians, and reports from the many commissions tasked with finding solutions for Canada's pressing problems—almost all of these commissions are named after the men that chaired them. In other words, this history is largely based on the accounts of those who are presented as prominent historical figures. This is one way of telling a story.

Canada's housing policy history is mostly told from this perspective. Take, for example, a 2017 *Maclean's* article on the release of the National Housing Strategy (NHS), which reads:

> With the announcement of his national housing strategy on Wednesday, Justin Trudeau has signalled the return to an era of federal housing responsibility—a bygone legacy of his father's. . . . While the federal government has had a role in housing since the mid-1930s, the program thrived from the late 60s to the early 90s. The period marked a shift towards non-profit and co-op housing, as the feds took a more active role in making

> sure Canadians had access to affordable homes. Between
> 1973 and 1993, 600,000 new units were added to sub-
> sidized housing stock, which the feds funded through
> agreements with housing providers. . . . In 1996, under
> Jean Chrétien, the Liberal government ended all funding
> for social housing, and downloaded responsibility for
> existing and new housing onto the provinces.[5]

The article goes on to quote experts who criticize the new strategy's investment amounts before it ends on a positive note, "but it's a heck of a good start." The photo accompanying the story features Prime Minister Justin Trudeau in profile, looking pensive as another man points to redevelopments charts on a wall. The message is clear: Pierre Trudeau led the country in the right direction by building the housing Canada needed. Then there were a few wrong turns, a blip. The son returns, thankfully taking the lead once again to move the country forward.

This may be just a magazine article, but that is how most people encounter history, through brief references to the past made here and there in media sources. Few have the luxury of carefully studying a specific topic, and even those who do are likely to stumble into similar narratives. In an academic article titled "The Reluctant Urbanist: Pierre Trudeau and the Creation of the Ministry of State for Urban Affairs," historian Zachary Spicer describes the creation of the federal ministry, which, at the time, some saw as part of the solution for pressing urban issues, including housing. The opening paragraph mentions "scores of urban activists and urban policy advocates"[6] calling for change as part of the political context, but of the 48 paragraphs in the article, three focus on these activists and the rest is devoted to Paul Hellyer, Robert Stanfield, and other prominent politicians pushing Pierre Trudeau to do the right thing. One of the tactics Stanfield used was going around the country and speaking "in front of crowds of urban activists, chastising Trudeau and openly contesting the Trudeauvian view of federalism."[7]

There we have it: two great men with strong ideas about the nation's future in an open battle in the public square. They are surrounded by crowds of activists playing the background actor roles that historians frequently assign them. Instead of describing the demands of social movements, the author chose to quote Stanfield's speeches at length. The crowd is anonymous and voiceless, whereas whatever that man said is worth repeating 40 years later. This, and other similar studies, are based on thorough research, and they pass rigorous peer reviews before publication. They are not wrong, but they tell only one side of the country's history. As urban geographer Pierson Nettling puts it, "Canadian studies have sought to understand housing through the elites."[8] If tenants are at all mentioned, their activism is relegated to a secondary role in the policy-making processes on which the studies centre. "The efforts of low-income people, labour unions, and social activists continue to be written out of Canadian policy studies."[9]

Historians like Alvin Finkel, Ian McKay, Georges Campeau, and Bryan D. Palmer, among others, take a different approach to history. They have studied how unions, social movements, and popular groups challenged and resisted the political agenda of the country's economic elites.[10] Researchers connected to labour and social movements have also produced accounts of their struggles.[11]

François Salliant, housing activist and former coordinator of the Front d'action populaire en réaménagement urbain (FRAPRU), wrote *Lutter pour un toit: Douze batailles pour le logement au Quebéc*, a must-read for anyone interested in tenant organizing.[12] Yutaka Dirks, social justice organizer and former outreach coordinator for the Advocacy Centre for Tenants Ontario, wrote an account of the organizing and coalition building behind recent campaigns for the right to housing.[13] The Right to Remain project connects historical research and organizing in a exceptional way.[14] The *Radical Housing Journal* has created a space for accounts of struggles that don't feature in the media or traditional academic journals.[15]

These authors and accounts paint a different picture of social and economic policies in Canada. They focus less on elite gentlemen who keenly argue about the country's future at some Ottawa château and more on common people gearing up to resist whatever comes out of those meetings, people whose interests never make it past the coat check. These stories are rarely told.

To sum up, capital owns history too. Not the real history, the history of common people, in common places, in common and extraordinary circumstances, but the recorded history that is told aloud, taught to children, and reproduced by mainstream culture. This history is capital's most precious asset. It gives the property-owning class the power to define what is possible and what is not.

History, when told from the perspective of the elite, presents a skewed view of the winners and losers of economic development. It assigns the capitalist class and its political representatives the role of leaders in shaping the country's future, with everyone else assigned secondary and passive roles. Learning and disseminating the stories of social groups not included in the dominant historical narrative is an important aspect of class struggle. It broadens the realm of possibility and highlights the agency and power of non-elite groups, like tenants, whose long tradition of defying the owing class is both remarkable and inspiring. Here I focus on a few pieces of *that* history.

TENANT STRUGGLES: A CANADIAN TRADITION

Accounts of tenant organizing centred on popular movements tell fascinating stories of tenants putting up fights across the country since before Confederation. This other side of housing policy history should be shared widely, included in secondary and post-secondary curricula, and forged into the country's collective memory. This would help address the cultural marginalization of the tenant class by promoting a positive view of hard-working families who have long fought to keep a fair share of their income.

More widespread knowledge of this history would also improve public debates about housing policy; among other things, it would challenge the "housing crisis" narrative, which is inaccurate, misleading, and unhelpful. Finally, organizers may find these stories helpful when calling other tenants to join the historical struggle against the landlord class, which includes many inspiring victories. The four abridged accounts below—Prince Edward Island (1860s), Nova Scotia (1930s), Montreal (1960s), and Vancouver (1970s)—provide a small sample of this remarkable history.

Prince Edward Island, 1864 to 1878

Before colonial settlement, the Mi'kmaq occupied the land that later became known as Prince Edward Island. The Europeans brought diseases that decimated between 50 and 90 percent of the Mi'kmaq population on the Atlantic coast. Then, British settlers proceeded to kill, dispossess, and deport them. By the 1870s, the surviving Mi'kmaq were confined to small areas the Crown had designed as reserves, from where they continued the fight against dispossession.[16] Around that time, another fight was picking up between two groups of settlers: those who owned land and those who rented. Landlords and tenants.

Canadian historian Ian Ross Robertson, born in Mermaid, Prince Edward Island, wrote a detailed study of the tenant movement that changed the land tenure system on the island, titled *The Tenant League of Prince Edward Island, 1864–1867*.[17] Other historians credited this book with shining a light on one of the popular movements overlooked in historical accounts of Confederation, which generally focus on parliamentary debates.[18]

Robertson explains that in 1767, the British Crown parcelled the island into 66 lots and distributed them through a lottery system to "political or military figures, or merchants with an already established interest in the region," most of whom resided in Great Britain.[19] The Crown assumed grantees would move to Prince Edward Island and tend to their properties, but few ever did. Grantees did not send family or trusted stewards either, because they considered the island too hostile and underdeveloped. "Proprietors therefore relied on the local elite for agents. . . . That colonial elite consisted, for the most part, of opportunistic individuals who had come to the New World to make their fortunes by hook or by crook."[20] The agents' job consisted of negotiating leases with tenants, collecting rents, and shipping the profits to Great Britain, where gentlefolk, who could not bother getting their shoes dirty, benefited from the hard work of tenant farmers they had never met. (REITs are not an original idea after all; landlords have long exploited tenants from afar.)

Lease terms provided landlords with low-risk high returns while subjecting tenants to high costs with few guarantees. The tenants' rent covered the landlords' taxes and other costs associated with owning the property, plus a comfortable profit margin. Tenants had to clear forests, build a house for themselves, and make the necessary improvements to turn virgin plots into agricultural land. They did all the work and covered all the costs, but if they were evicted or their lease was not renewed, they were forced to walk away from everything they built.

Rent prices were set in sterling instead of the local currency. The customary exchange rate for rent payment was 1:1.11, but landlords had the legal right to use a higher exchange rate, 1:1.50, which was the rate applied in other commercial activities. "The exercise of this prerogative appears to have been capricious," notes Robertson, "and could most frequently be accounted for by the tyrannical disposition of an unusually harsh landlord or agent or by a specific conflict with a particular tenant."[21] Landlords used the right to apply different exchange rates and substantially increase the price of rent as a way to threaten and punish defiant tenants, who could have their life's work taken away, sometimes overnight, by people who had never touched a plow.

Tenants eventually had enough and went on strike. On May 19, 1864, "seventy to eighty delegates and friends of the emerging tenant movement met" and agreed on two actions: challenge a recently approved piece of legislation and organize The Tenant Union of Prince Edward Island, widely known as the Tenant League. The movement organized local committees in every township on the island; their initial task was to decide upon a "fair and reasonable price" to buy out landlords. In leasehold tenure systems, land is rarely sold to third parties; usually, it is transferred within kin groups. In this context, tenants stating their intention to buy the land and setting the price they were willing to pay for it was a big slap in the face to the landlord class. The Tenant's Pledge approved at the union's convention also included a rent strike: signatories committed to "withhold the further liquidation or rent and arrears of rents."[22]

In a public statement, the Tenant League estimated its membership surpassed eleven thousand members.

Landlords counterattacked. Their first action was the most obvious one, which continues to be employed by landlords today: threatening tenants in arrears with legal evictions. It did not work. The fight escalated, and landlords did what they often do in these situations: they called on the state to protect their interests. The police went after the Tenant League's leaders, and the government declared the Tenant League an illegal organization. Eventually, Halifax sent troops to the island to ensure order and collect rents, but League members managed to convince a share of the deployed troops to defect. Despite this, tenants were overpowered by the Crown's troops. Small wins continued over the next decade, with the piecemeal purchase of land and the slow turning of the island into a freehold tenure system. In 1878, Prince Edward Island, now part of the Dominion of Canada, passed legislation dispossessing absentee landlords.

Once the island became the responsibility of Ottawa, the Mi'kmaq tried to reclaim their land, but with the passing of the Indian Act (1876), the Canadian government continued and deepened the colonization process the Crown had started. Settlers, tenants, and landlords alike benefited from this process. Reconciling a class-based struggle against landlords and the ongoing fight for decolonization remains a challenge for today's tenant movements—the Vancouver Tenants Union (VTU) is one example of a tenant group trying to find ways to do so.

Nova Scotia, 1917 to 1949

On the tragic morning of December 6, 1917, a munitions ship leaving the Halifax harbour collided with another ship, detonating two and a half tonnes of explosives, killing two thousand people, injuring another nine thousand, and devasting an entire section of the north end of the city—the home of hundreds of working-class tenant families. Following the Halifax explosion, a relief commission tasked with rebuilding efforts replaced the destroyed rental homes with better quality, publicly owned, working-class rental homes—approximately 345 houses in a neighbourhood known as The Hydrostone.[23]

The experts leading the commission adhered to planning ideas popular in England at the time, implementing their vision of what a working-class neighbourhood should look like. Along the way, tenants challenged these experts' choices by arguing they were unacquainted with local realities. "Just imagine," said one tenant, "kitchens, which was the poor man's principal room being but eight feet square. After a table and a stove were put in there was no room for a flour barrel or groceries."[24] Tenants and labour movement activists demanded a more democratic process, but the relief commission had extraordinary emergency powers that allowed it to ignore such complaints. Despite the undemocratic, top-down approach, at least the focus was right. The Hydrostone was designed as non-market working-class housing, with the rental income funding a public pension plan.[25]

This overall positive approach to reconstruction was not extended to earlier inhabitants. Settlers had aggressively pushed the Mi'kmaq out of the land that became the Halifax port area. By 1907, only a few Mi'kmaq families lived in a seasonal settlement along the Dartmouth shore called Turtle Grove, comprised of seven wigwams and a school. This settlement was destroyed by the tsunami resulting from the explosion, and it was never rebuilt. Instead, the explosion was used as an opportunity to deport the remaining Mi'kmaq. Today, the area is named

Tufts Cove, after the family that treated the Mi'kmaq as squatters and demanded their forced removal.[26]

By the early 1930s, urban planners advising the province's Housing Committee were not committed to working-class rental houses; instead, they argued the government should launch a campaign to educate workers on the benefits of homeownership. But if urban planners moved on to another policy fad, housing militants continued to fight for good quality, non-market rental homes for working-class Haligonians. Over the next decades, social housing remained the focus of grassroots activism, with the labour movement playing a crucial role in pushing this agenda.

In March 1931, the Labour Council's newspaper, the *Citizen*, announced the launch of a campaign for low-income rental housing. They warned the "greedy dabblers in real estate, [and] hungry landlords who thrive on human poverty and want,"[27] that organized labour was gearing up for a battle. The Labour Council created a housing committee of its own to develop policy proposals, launch a public housing campaign, encourage union members to learn about the wicked housing system, and actively participate in the province's Citizen Housing Committee, where it pressed for a provincial Housing Commission (the Commission).

In late 1931, the provincial government announced the creation of such commission, but then it took almost two years to appoint the Commission and start the works. Labour representatives were excluded from the Commission, with preference given to better-behaved civil society organizations. Not being in the room to rub shoulders with urban planners and politicians did not prevent labour militants from pushing for non-market housing. In an examination of public housing in Halifax—which focuses not only on policy debates but also on popular movements—Canadian historian John C. Bacher argued that, "although professional, religious and social service groups participated in the housing crusade, the labour movement in the city was critical in sustaining the campaign for improved low-income housing."[28] This was because organized labour's interest in rental housing "continued when that of other sectors of the community lagged or fell dormant."[29]

~~In 1949, Nova Scotia became one of the first provinces to sign up for a federal program to build social housing.~~ It was an overly complicated program that produced a modest number of units, mostly in places where political demand was strong enough.[30] Still, the prompt and active participation of Nova Scotia should be seen as a victory for tenant activism, which succeeded in keeping public housing alive in the political imaginary. Urban planning fads came and went. Progressive bureaucrats pushed public housing, until they moved on to other jobs. Experts joined endless panels tasked with drafting a plan to plan. In turn, tenant militants kept the fight alive, with the support of organized labour, who understood rental housing to be a pivotal working-class struggle and served as a pillar for the tenant movement.

Montreal, Quebec, 1966 to 1970

Across the world, large-scale evictions and displacements have been carried out on behalf of "urban renewal." The specific programs vary from place to place, as does the language used to justify them, but the core idea behind urban renewal is straightforward: clear out old buildings and precarious dwellings and build something shiny and modern in their place. Projects meant to "restore economic viability" may involve transforming apartment buildings into high-income condos and shopping outlets.

Initiatives aimed at addressing "urban decay" will likely
bulldoze areas labelled "slums," forcefully displacing their
residents. Large "land redevelopments" may replace entire
neighbourhoods with megaprojects deemed good for the
economy—like an Olympic Park.

In the heyday of state-sponsored urban renewal in
North America (1950s to 1960s), many of these projects
promised the construction of new, public, and affordable
rental housing. Sometimes these promises came true; other
times, affordable housing fell by the wayside. Where it was
built, the question became how public housing was managed, for urban renewal ideology is not only about clean-
ing urban spaces but also about controlling low-income
tenants, making sure they behave like middle-class folk.

In the post-war period, provincial and municipal governments proudly spearheaded urban renewal projects in
the name of progress and economic development, often
using federal funding to pay for them. After a while, the
collateral damage became visible and political consensus
around these projects weakened. In 1969, federal cabinet
minister Paul Hellyer chaired the committee that drafted a
proposal for a different, more cautious approach to urban
revitalization. This document—known as the *Hellyer
Report*, naturally—is widely credited for putting an end to
federal government support for urban renewal initiatives.[31]
But as is usually the case, this story has other, less-known
aspects.

In one of those uncommon studies of social policy that
shine a light on overlooked and disregarded popular movements, urban geographer Pierson Nettling argued that
Montreal's tenant movement played a significant role in
challenging the consensus around urban renewal policies.[32]
In 1954, the City of Montreal, a keen adopter of urban
renewal, partnered with the Central Mortgage Housing

Corporation on a project to build public housing through "slum" clearance, which would also expand the city's business district. The project involved the demolition of the red-light district and parts of Chinatown and the displacement of the LGBTQ community. But, in this case, public housing was actually built: a 796-unit complex of modern row houses and apartment towers, called Habitations Jeanne-Mance (HJM), was completed in 1961.

Then there was the second aspect of urban renewal: the disciplining of tenants. Residents had to sign a rental contract containing 32 punitive clauses. Though a federal government requirement, the authority to enforce these rules was endowed to a local administrator. This was too much authority in the view of the tenants that launched, in 1966, the Comité des Citoyens des Habitations Jeanne-Mance (the Comité). One of their first actions was a press release denouncing the living conditions in HJM, perceived injustices in the rent scale, corrupted management practices, and the surveillance of tenants by maintenance personnel. According to Nettling, this was the first collective action against urban renewal policies.

The administrator, Léopold Rogers, fiercely responded to tenant activism. He swiftly evicted the author of the press release, tenant organizer Napoléan Saint-André. In his archival research, Nettling found it was not uncommon for the administrator to evict tenants, with a five-day notice, for participation in political activities. Rogers didn't stop there. "Rogers allegedly bribed Gérald Lalonde, the head priest at Saint Jacques Catholic Church—where the majority Catholic population went to worship—to disclose their weekly confessions." He later argued this was done to improve the behaviour of the poor. Other intimidation tactics included demanding tenants to withdraw from all associations and political organizations or be evicted.

requiring the meetings of any social group within the HJM to be preapproved; persecuting organizers in other spheres of their lives; and appointing a co-opted tenant representative to the HJM board instead of someone from the Comité.

The Comité pushed forward despite surveillance and retaliation. In addition to exposing the realities at HJM and tarnishing the public view of urban renewal, members of the Comité forged alliances with other activist groups and launched an offshoot community-based political group called Mouvement pour justice sociale (MJS). In subsequent years, the Comité and MJS fought against the gendered definition of "family" that put widows at risk of eviction since they were considered "people living alone" and, as such, not eligible for HJM housing. Other actions leading to increased public scrutiny in the management of HJM eventually led to Rogers's resignation. (Before leaving, he fired a social worker who had sided with tenant organizers). In 1967, Comité members disrupted a City Council meeting for more than two hours in protest of the lack of tenant representation in the board of directors that managed the HJM.

After a few years of the creation of the Comité and the MJS, the relationship between tenant-based movements and Montreal's left became complicated. Through interviews and archival research, Nettling learned about a cleavage in housing activism. Segments of the left blamed poor living conditions at HJM on the design of large public housing projects. These were mostly "progressive" intellectuals and urban planner types, some of whom became openly anti-HJM, joining conservatives in deeming these "ghettos" an urban planning failure.

Hellyer, too, was against not only urban renewal but public housing generally, though that is less-often cited.[34]

In contrast, militant tenants focused on governance questions, denouncing the surveillance and disciplining aspects of urban renewal, and organizing actions to improve living conditions. While experts were willing to throw the baby out with the bathwater and move on to the next policy fad, tenants worried about concrete problems.

~~Nettling concluded that "the Comité effectively developed an alternative perspective to housing that countered the New Left-conservative consensus on the pathologies of public housing design. How tenants built this alternative was through class politics."[35]~~ Similar tensions can be found in today's movements. Parkdale Organize, for example, was created partly as a response to its members' disillusionment with Toronto's left and its inability to focus on the struggles of working-class people.

To date, HJM remains one of the oldest public housing projects in the country. Over the decades, several people fought to make HJM a publicly owned and democratically run alternative to market housing. Oddly, its name symbolizes just the opposite. Jeanne Mance was a French settler and one of the co-founders of Ville-Marie (Montreal). Her feats included travelling to France to raise funds to build a hospital, funds she first lent to Paul de Chomedey de Maisonneuve—French settler, military, developer, and co-founder of Montreal—who used the money to build a militia to battle the Iroquois people resisting colonization. As recent as 2017, the agency that manages HJM released a brochure where Jeanne-Mance and Maisonneuve are celebrated as the pious and courageous people that founded Montreal.[36] French settlers led the privatization of land through the dispossession of Indigenous Peoples, paving the way to profit-making in housing—the very problem HJM tries to address.

Vancouver, British Columbia, 1968 to 1978

British Columbia has a strong tradition of militant tenant organizing. 1968 to 1978 is an important chapter of this history, where broad and strong tenant organizing resulted in important victories—even though some battles were lost. In the years leading up to this period, the absence of rent controls fuelled frequent, localized, and short-lived organizing against abusive landlords. In 1968, after losing a dispute against a 5 percent rent increase in their apartment complex, the Driftwood Tenants' Association (DTA) spearheaded the creation of the Vancouver Tenant Council (VTC).[37] In the words of one of the organizers, "we didn't win that battle but we did establish the fact that tenants were determined to get organized and make their voices heard."[38] The VTC was a broader and more permanent organization; it charged tenants a \$2 annual membership fee (\$16 in 2022), allowing it to pay for an office with a phone line.[39]

The VTC continued to support local disputes against abusive landlords but also took on the municipal government. At the time, municipal governments in BC regulated most rental housing matters. In 1969, the VTC and allied city councillors made significant gains by passing a bylaw that introduced a series of new regulations: a maximum of one rent increase per year; mandatory three months' notice of rent increases; a \$25 limit on security deposits; and making landlords responsible for repairs.[40] For Bruce Yorke, a housing activist and Vancouver city councillor at the time, the bylaw did not strengthen tenant representation in landlord and tenant boards, but at least it "set the stage for continued activity of the tenant movement."[41]

In 1970, the VTC joined forces with tenant associations in Burnaby, New Westminster, Surrey, North Vancouver, Victoria, and Campbell River, forming the BC Tenants'

Organization (BCTO). Together, they pushed for revising the province's Landlord and Tenant Act, which dates back to before Confederation and bears outdated language and concepts from a time when tenants rented farmland. It provided many rights to landlords and practically no protections for tenants.

Ontario had revised its residential tenancy act in 1968, drawing on a law reform commission that reviewed the matter in detail. In particular, the Ontario commission argued that tenants should have the right to collective bargaining as the asymmetric power relations between tenants and landlords would prevent fair outcomes in grievance cases and other negotiations—much like in the case of workers and bosses. Similarly, the BCTO made collective bargaining rights a central demand.

The election platform of the 1972-elected New Democratic Party (NDP) government included a commitment to collective bargaining rights for tenants, but the party eventually backed down on this promise. According to Yorke, the party was "afraid of the economic power of large real estate and corporate interests."[42] To add insult to injury, the NDP government created a Rentalsman Office that, much like present-day landlord and tenant boards, painted a veneer of legitimacy and impartiality to dispute processes stacked up in favour of landlords. Yorke explains: "Since the rentalsman concept was introduced, the tenant movement had become steadily weaker, and no doubt that was one of the reasons why this concept was introduced and bargaining rights for tenants were never introduced."[43]

The final 1974 Landlord and Tenant Act cemented the many substantive victories made at the municipal level. Landlords won the battle on bargaining rights, but BC tenants set an enormously valuable precedent for what was, and continues to be, one of the most important aspects of

the struggle: the recognition that tenants should have political rights, including the right to bargain collectively.

———————————

There were many other tenant struggles over the past
century. "Winnipeg was a bastion of housing activism"
in the 1960s and 1970s.[44] The Indian and Metis Tenants
Association fought for the rights of Indigenous tenants,
and the Winnipeg Tenant Association helped push for
the Manitoba public housing construction boom.[45] In the
1970s, Toronto tenants also played a crucial role in creating the political moment for rent controls in Ontario. Other
examples exist. Despite the importance of documenting
them all, that is too big of a task for this short book. For
now, these selected examples and abridged accounts suffice
to remind that Canadian history—the real history of common people—has numerous cases of tenants organizing as
a class and wielding collective power.

   The struggle continues today, with clear ties with the
past, but also changes that require tenant movements to
craft new tactics to confront a landlord class that continues
to grow stronger, politically and economically.

CHAPTER FIVE

Tenant Organizing Today

Today, tenants across Canada continue to organize, build communities and solidary networks, take on abusive landlords, oppose rent increases, demand repairs, resist evictions, and block redevelopment and displacement plans. Organize, resist, repeat. Thousands of tenants do this every day, before and after work, on weekends, with a child in one arm and a pot on the stove. They organize in tenant unions, neighbourhood groups, *comités logement*, and tenant-based coalitions.

The remarkable organizing work of tenant groups is an inspiring example of class-based struggles and the continuation of Canada's long tradition of tenant resistance and power.[1] The distinctive feature of tenant groups is the clear-eyed understanding that gross socioeconomic inequality is a constitutive aspect of housing markets. Some people and businesses benefit enormously from housing markets and don't want the so-called housing crisis ever to end. If they were to have their way, there would be even fewer regulations on rental housing and more opportunities for profit maximization. Since these groups have a lot of economic and political influence, the people getting the short end of the stick—tenants—cannot expect conditions to improve on their own. In the words of Bruno Dobrusin, a York South-Weston Tenant Union member, "we either organize ourselves and confront landlords, or we succumb to their whims; no one is coming for us."[2] Tenant groups organize to build power to defend the interests of tenants and working-class families against landlords and the political system that backs them up.

The most direct and sure way to contribute to the tenant struggle is to join one of these groups, at your building, neighbourhood, or city. Or start one. Organizing principles, tactics, day-to-day actions, and long-term strategies always vary from tenant group to tenant group. These decisions can only be made locally and by the people involved. Still, it is valuable to describe organizing approaches and share examples of disputes won and lost so tenants everywhere know collective action is not only possible, it's happening now.

As a researcher, my organizing experience consists mostly of moving around decimal points and semicolons, and I don't pretend otherwise. For this reason, the following sections draw directly and quote heavily from accounts written by tenant union members and interviews with them.

RENT-STRIKING THE REIT

The growth of REITs poses both challenges and opportunities for tenant organizing. On the one hand, the economic strength of financial investors takes the unequal power dynamics between tenants and landlords to another level; the sheer number of resources a REIT can deploy in any, and every, dispute with tenants is unmatchable. On the other hand, REITs rely on a good public profile to sell shares to investors; bad press in one building can affect an entire portfolio, making these landlords vulnerable to bad press in ways other landlords are not. REITs also become predictable as their actions against tenants in one place are shared with tenants elsewhere, which helps organizers to plan.

Tenants in Hamilton organized a rent strike in buildings owned by one of the country's largest REITs. In 2017, InterRent bought four buildings in Riverdale, a neighbourhood that has long served as a destination for immigrant families. The high cost of housing in Toronto (60 kilometres away) and transportation improvements that make commuting to the big city easier have made Riverdale an ideal target for gentrification. Soon after the acquisition, InterRent announced a 9 percent rent increase. The seven-month strike that ensued "was an intense roller-coaster ride for tenants as well as organizers with ups and downs, thrills and scares, joy and fatigue."[3] In collaboration with a postdoctoral fellow conducting participatory action research, one of the Hamilton Tenants Solidarity Network (HTSN) members documented this experience. Here are some excerpts from their story:

> [HTSN] is a volunteer, grassroots group composed of tenants. While we have a larger base of supporters, a core group of nine organizers was involved in the recent rent strike campaign. People of various political stripes are part of the group, but we are broadly anti-capitalist and anti-authoritarian. Our goal is to build independent working-class power, with a focus on densely populated neighbourhoods that have a high concentration of renters.[4]

In the months leading up to the strike, HTSN canvassed the four buildings (618 units) InterRent had just bought, collecting information about the tenants (languages spoken for example), recent rent increases, and above-guideline rent increase (AGI) applications. They also assessed people's interest in participating in committee meetings.

In the lead-up to and during the rent strike, Tenant Committee meetings became more regular and attendance increased. At the peak of the strike, we had monthly mass meetings (for tenants from all four buildings), weekly lobby meetings (in each of the four buildings), and bi-weekly "strike captains" meetings, with the most involved strikers from each of the buildings. . . . Tenants have voted on all the big decisions, about going on rent strike in the first place, and later about the direction of the rent strike.[5]

Meanwhile, HTSN sought legal advice on the potential consequences of withholding rent. They treaded carefully, and, in the end, no tenant was displaced due to the strike.[6] HTSN also had a communications plan: "We think it is important to engage mainstream media as this has the potential to raise the profile of a campaign, publicly shame the landlord, amplify tenants' demands, generate community support, and introduce a radical vision of tenant resistance to a broader audience." Other social events and political actions were also part of the strike.

Tenants celebrated the launch of the rent strike by sharing a potluck meal at the local park, marching through the neighbourhood, making speeches, and dropping a large "RENT STRIKE!" banner from the top floor of one of the buildings. In the strike's first month, tenants held a rally and delivered a large stack of work order forms to the property manager's office, documenting a slew of longstanding maintenance issues in their apartments and demanding that they be addressed. In June [2018], tenants travelled to the financial district in Toronto to visit the office of CI Financial, the largest investor in InterRent, and demanded that the company withdraw its investments in InterRent (which they didn't do, unfortunately). [7]

The HTSN member who documented this struggle avowed that the organization underestimated how important it was for InterRent to negotiate within the standard Landlord and Tenant Board framework and not set a precedent by negotiating directly with the rent strikers or succumbing to their demands. In their view, "InterRent seemed intent on crushing the rent strike to set an example for the burgeoning tenant movement in Ontario and to protect their investment strategy."[8]

Organizers in Toronto, Vancouver, and Ottawa also mentioned financial and corporate landlords' conscious efforts not to set a precedent by caving to tenant demands. While this strategic choice exemplifies their economic might and ability to sustain short-term losses for long-term returns, it is also a sign of their fear that word of tenant power spreads. As with capitalists everywhere, landlords dread the rise of class consciousness.

In the end, the landlord did not drop the rent increase, but the Landlord and Tenant Board approved a reduced AGI. Demands for repairs were also met. "Beyond this, tenants have a renewed sense of dignity and pride in their homes, know more of their neighbours, meet regularly to discuss common concerns and plans of action, and have established a strong basis of trust and solidarity."[9]

After five years of activity, the HTSN dissolved in February 2020. The statement of dissolution explained that members had opted to focus on localized neighbourhood activities rather than on attempting to build a city-wide organization. They concluded this would be a more

effective and long-term power-building strategy. "We hope
that tenants across the city will continue this fight," the
letter stated.[10]

The neighbourhood-level versus city-wide organizing
debate is a common one. Battles happen at the local level.
When landlords issue eviction and rent increase notices,
neighbours either stand together to fight them or they
don't. It makes a lot of sense to focus on building power
locally, because those notices will come, and when they do,
politicians, policy wonks, and progressive researchers will
be nowhere to be seen. On the other hand, in many contexts, labour and other social movements made important
gains by combining local-level organizing and the forming
of broader political coalitions. In the end, this is one of the
strategic choices that only the people directly involved can
make.

TERRITORIAL ORGANIZING

Abusive landlords are not the only enemy. Tenants confront cultural and economic injustices in the labour market, vis-à-vis the state, in relations with some of their
neighbours, and within their own households. Whether
to focus exclusively on tenant issues or organize around
all working-class disputes within an area is a founda-
tional political and strategic decision. Parkdale Organize
(Toronto), a neighbourhood group that receives no funding
and has no staff, has been deliberate about this decision,
focusing on all working-class struggles within their neighbourhood. As two group members explain: "In the group's
six-year history [Parkdale Organize] has contributed to the
struggles of working-class people against landlords, bosses,
and the state, including high-profile rent strikes involving
hundreds of Parkdale tenants."[11]

Parkdale Organize stands out as having a clearly

articulated political project, which seems to result from much reflection and internal debate.

> We began having political discussions about territorial organizing as early as 2012. Our years of experience with the Left had disillusioned us with prevalent approaches to organizing and we started looking for new strategies. We concluded that political intervention within a specific territory of the city presented the greatest potential for the construction of independent working-class organizations. We saw an opportunity to make interventions to open up and defend new spaces for the development of working-class organizations that were independent from non-profit and Left hegemony. The founding members of Parkdale Organize were tenants or workers in the Parkdale neighbourhood. Residence and employment in the neighbourhood provided a vantage point to begin to know and understand Parkdale's social conditions. This "on the ground" perspective coupled with a shared understanding of the failures of the historic and contemporary Left was the basis for our earliest political interventions, eventually leading to the formation of Parkdale Organize. . . . [12]
>
> Tenant unions, labour unions, migrant rights, and homeless and anti-poverty organizing purport to represent specific sectors of the working class or broader society. A tenant union organizes around "tenant issues" such as rents and evictions. Its political outlook is to improve conditions for tenants. Parkdale Organize intervenes on the struggles of working-class people in Parkdale. We don't aim to organize within any particular sector of the economy. Instead, we aim to intervene within the myriad of struggles facing working-class people within a particular territory. We aim to build the

power of working-class people, as a class, within that
territory.[13]

Tenant struggles are a major focus for Parkdale
Organize because the reality of the area demands it. In
Parkdale, 87 percent of households rent, compared to
47 percent in Toronto. Participation in the labour market (71 percent) is also higher than the average for the
city (65 percent). In other words, this is predominantly a
working-class tenant population.[14] Parkdale is near both
Lake Ontario and High Park (one of the city's largest and
oldest parks), while only six kilometres from the downtown core, in a straight line served by public transit. This
privileged location has put the area on the map of wealthy
families and developers who have tried to push the working class out for more than a century. They continue trying,
as there is good money to be made.[15]

Of the many Parkdale Organize actions and disputes
with landlords, bosses, and the state, a 2017 rent strike that
mobilized more than 300 tenants stands out. In January
of that year, corporate landlord MetCap notified tenants
at 87 Jameson Avenue of an above-guideline increase that
would push rents up by an average of $150 a month over
three years. Tenants reached out to Parkdale Organize, and
a strong resistance was mounted for months. In the end,
MetCap had to sit with the strikers and negotiate. "Over
the course of two meetings, a settlement agreement was
reached which significantly reduced the rent increases and
provided further rent relief to tenants on fixed incomes."[16]

In 2020, a corporate landlord refused to negotiate the
arrears of a single mother in an apartment building in the
nearby neighbourhood of Little Portugal. She and her children faced eviction and likely homelessness, amid a global
pandemic, during the winter. Twenty Parkdale Organize

members came over one morning, mobilized other tenants in the building, and forced the landlord to call off the eviction.[17] In 2022, the group stopped the eviction of an entire 23-unit building. The organizing work started two years earlier, upon tenants learning the building had been acquired by a corporate landlord who would likely try to "reposition" the property. During the pandemic, tenants build solidarity by meeting regularly and supporting each other in various ways. When the eviction notices came in 2022, they were ready.

> Tenants immediately responded by delivering a letter as a group to the landlords at their homes demanding that the eviction notices be withdrawn within one week. When the landlords did not meet their demand, tenants hung banners from their balconies and spoke out in the media. When the landlords retaliated by issuing eviction notices alleging that hanging banners is an illegal act, tenants held firm and continued to press their demands. . . . Despite the landlords' attempts to single tenants out and to pick them off one by one, tenants remained united. Our neighbours at 12 Lansdowne know that organizing is what enables them to defend their homes.[18]

As Parkdale Organize's statement of principles puts it, "When working class people in Parkdale struggle, we have their backs."[19]

CHANGING CITY POLITICS

At some point, social movements have to decide where they stand on party politics, knowing they will likely be criticized no matter where they stand. Movements that choose to support political parties may be accused of betraying their base and the organizers of pursuing personal ambitions. Movements that stay out of party politics may be called naive or sectarian, and their organizers can be seen as unwilling to compromise for a greater cause. A movement that changes its position in response to a new political context can look unprincipled, whereas one that sticks to its plan may look intransigent. Damned if you do, damned if you don't. Ultimately, it is for movements to choose a course of action that works for their reality.

Among the different tenant groups, the York South-Weston Tenant Union stands out as having active and deliberate involvement with party politics. Here is more about them and their particular position, in their own words:

> We're a group of tenants and tenant associations in York South-Weston helping each other protect our tenant rights and reinforce communities of solidarities in this area. We are committed to:
> 1. Sharing information and resources about tenant rights to help reduce rent increases and get necessary repairs done.
> 2. Organizing and advocating for tenant rights and the fight to housing in our community. The York South-Weston Tenants' Union covers the area south of the 401, north of St Clair Ave, between the Humber River, and the rail line just to the east of Keele Street. It organizes 13 different tenant associations in this territory. Choosing the political-electoral riding as a context is a choice directly related to engagement with the political process.[20]

Readers who know Toronto will likely recognize the York South-Weston Tenants' Union perimeter as the fringe between two worlds: affluent, gentrified downtown neighbourhoods like Bloor West Village; and the city's inner suburbs, comprised mainly of middle-income detached houses and high-rise apartment buildings, like Rexdale. Toronto's City Council is roughly divided between progressive downtown councillors and conservative inner-suburb councillors. York South-Weston (YSW) does not easily fit into either camp.

> YSW, and tenant issues in particular, are not on the map of Toronto politics. We hear the downtown versus suburb stuff all the time, and it doesn't speak to our reality. Downtown is a faraway place for children in these neighbourhoods, but we don't all have the same experiences as people growing up north or east of here, further out. We're a bit of both. Most tenants in our community don't interact with downtown, more often than not they go to work in industrial areas in the broader [Greater Toronto Area].
>
> Public transit is a good example. People here don't think a car is absolutely necessary like other parts of the city. We can get to places using transit; many tenants take the subway to work. But we have to get to the subway first, and it is not a couple of blocks away like downtown. In the whole subways versus cars debate, our demand is always for more buses, bus rapid lanes, and the integration of transit passes. We are crossed by one of the best, yet most expensive and exclusive transit systems in the city, the UP Express [train service connecting the downtown to the airport]. But most of us don't think of using it on a daily basis, since it's almost double the cost of the TTC [subway/bus/streetcar network] and it is not even integrated, which means we have to pay another bus or subway fare when we connect.[21]

YSW is in a city ward that has had the same councillor since the 1980s when Frances Nunziata was elected councillor and then later the mayor of York. Once York became part of Toronto, she became the area's Toronto councillor—and the rest is history. Against this backdrop, York South-Weston Tenant Union's political project includes casting out Nunziata, taking over her seat, and challenging the dominant narrative in city politics that places homeowners as the sole constituency worth listening to.

Nobody stays in office that long without rewarding supporters and punishing challengers, and that's what we see here. Service providers and traditional community groups mean well, and they have helped tenants in the past, but when push comes to shove, they will not confront the councillor. No matter what she does or how little she does, they don't confront her for fear of the repercussions. People are afraid of getting on her wrong side. We're not. Nunziata's core supporters are the biggest landlords in our area. We know what side she is on, so we have to build alternatives that confront this reality.

The City has many powers that could be put to use to help tenants. Not sending the police to "keep the peace" during evictions is one of them; regulating rooming houses would also make a difference; ensuring City-subsidized housing is actually affordable would be nice, even if that is not a long-term solution. The city could use the powers of expropriation to put forward more housing capacity for low-income tenants. But when our councillor is siding with landlords and developers, all of this is a nonstarter.[22]

One of the union's organizers, Chiara Padovani, ran

for council in 2018 and came in third place, with 20 percent of the votes. She ran again in 2022, receiving 47 percent of the votes this time, only 94 votes short of beating Nunziata. Another organizer ran in the 2019 federal election, but did not win. YSW organizers usually participate in electoral campaigns—which are extremely taxing on the group—as big picture power-building efforts and often reiterate the goal of putting YSW on the map.

> We believe that tenants need to have a collective voice and build collective power also in the electoral arena. That's why, on top of the organizing building by building that we do, we also use elections to organize and politicize tenants, to intervene in debates that will shape the realities we live in. We do this sometimes by running our own tenant candidates and other times by bringing tenant voices to the main issues that are debated in the electoral cycle.[23]

The York South-Weston Tenant Union's day-to-day focus is similar to that of other tenant groups: challenging rent increases, stopping evictions, getting repairs done, and organizing more buildings. In the words of Padovani, "We are up against developers and landlords with endless resources; we got to pull together like [labour] unions did; if we don't, we risk being crushed one at a time."[24]

COALITIONS OF TENANT GROUPS

Social movements make strategic decisions regarding how to support each other's struggles. In some cases, a local group contributes to groups elsewhere simply by sharing their experiences and providing an inspirational example. This is the case of Parkdale Organize, whose stories are known across the country. Sometimes, community-based groups turn into organizations with an administrative structure and local chapters, like the Association of Community Organizations for Reform Now (ACORN).

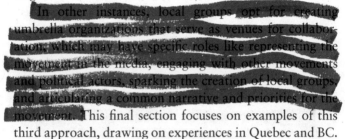

In other instances, local groups opt for creating umbrella organizations that serve as venues for collaboration, which may have specific roles like representing the movement in the media, engaging with other movements and political actors, sparking the creation of local groups, and articulating a common narrative and priorities for the movement. This final section focuses on examples of this third approach, drawing on experiences in Quebec and BC.

In the 1970s, Quebec tenants who had lived through the displacements associated with urban renewal projects like Habitations Jeanne-Mance had to contend with the latest public policy fad: neighbourhood improvement programs (Programmes d'amélioration de quartier, or PAQ). The federal and provincial governments funded these programs, while municipalities implemented them without much input from residents, which often led to gentrification and the displacement of low-income families. Neighbourhoods organized in response, creating *comités de quartier*, *comités logement*, and *associations de locataires*. In 1978, seven of these groups formed a rent freeze coalition that later became the Regroupement des comités logement et associations de locataires du Québec (RCLALQ).[25]

Also, in 1978, the participants of a grassroots conference on PAQ impacts voted in favour of creating an umbrella organization to change the power balance vis-à-vis the state and push for public programs that benefited their neighbourhoods. These groups wanted to do more than reacting to the nefarious impacts of government programs, and so the Front d'action populaire en réaménagement urbain (FRAPRU) was born.[26] The two organizations collaborated on many campaigns, and around 1983, they considered merging. However, RCLALQ was concerned with losing sight of its focus on rent controls, so they remained separate organizations that occasionally collaborated—they remain separate to this day.[27]

FRAPRU's structure is simple and democratic. Its 30 members gather in annual congresses to vote on yearly priorities, while a smaller administrative committee handles day-to-day tasks and urgent matters. Most of its members are *comités logement* and *comités d'action*: neighbourhood-level groups that support tenants in defending their rights while organizing them politically. Many of these groups also focus on popular education. FRAPRU has five full-time staff: one coordinator, one spokesperson, and three organizers. The organization participates in a broad range of spaces, from its grassroots base and interventions with the media to small group meetings with experts and elected officials.

In all of these different spaces, FRAPRU displays a resolute political perspective based on three guiding principles:

1. housing is a fundamental right;
2. profit-making is incongruent with the upholding of this fundamental right, thus the state must play a central role in housing, fostering a strong non-profit sector and regulating private actors; and
3. citizens should exercise greater control of housing and urban planning more broadly.

One of its recent brochures nicely summarizes these three principles, *Le logement: pas une merchandise. Un droit!*[28]

The RCLALQ has an equally inspiring 40-year history of struggles for tenant rights. Its current membership includes 53 tenant groups across the province of Quebec.

Rent control remains the top priority, but over the years other issues have been added: making the landlord-tenant boards a place where tenants can access justice; the fight against discrimination in housing; the fight against unhealthy living conditions; and protections against all types of evictions. In addition to continually pushing on these fronts, RCLALQ also organizes successful campaigns on timely issues, like its vigorous campaign for a ban on Airbnb (Quebec was the first province to regulate the online firm). RCLALQ also gets folks out on the streets, and its well-humoured demonstrations tend to capture public attention. For example, in 1997, during the "guilty of being poor in a rich society campaign," RCLALQ members did a deputation at the national assembly wearing inmate costumes. Overall, the RCLALQ seems to strike a nice balance between focusing on core issues and articulating broad political messages for the tenant movement.

The third and final example is the Vancouver Tenants Union (VTU). Founded in 2017, this city-wide union enlisted more than 2,500 members in only a few years. Tenants can join the union directly as individual members. Some members are part of local tenant groups and join to connect their group with the broader tenant movement, others come to the VTU first, then start local groups with the union's support. Other members join to contribute to city- and provincial-level political actions led by VTU.

In addition to joining as a general member or a member of a local chapter, people can join five action committees: Membership Organizing, Communications, Defend Broadway, and Data Tools. Members hash out priorities for the year at annual general meetings and elect a steering committee. Any member in good standing can vote and run—the suggested annual membership due is $1 per

$1,000 of annual income. At the time of writing, there were three active local chapters, and one of them, Mount Pleasant, recently had a large victory. In their own words:

> In the Fall of 2020, renters in Mount Pleasant and Vancouver faced off against the developer PortLiving and won. For years, PortLiving had been rapidly growing their property empire in the neighbourhood, displacing working class tenants as they developed luxury condos along the Broadway Corridor. The tenants of Mount Pleasant had had enough. We took on the developer and their allies in Vancouver City Staff knowing that the future of our community was at stake. . . .
>
> With less than 6 weeks to the eviction, members of the Mount Pleasant Chapter met every Sunday before flyering and postering across the neighbourhood, recruiting residents and retailers to defend the tenants' homes. Meanwhile, the Union's Communications Working Group worked tirelessly to collect hundreds of pledges from tenants across Vancouver to join the fight. . . .
>
> After holding the picket from 8AM to 6PM three straight days, the tenants won a stay of eviction in the courts [which stops the landlord from executing eviction for a fixed amount of time, giving tenants more time to find and move to another home]. This was a major victory for renters in Vancouver. . . .
>
> This fight was never just about the homes at Broadway–Carolina. In two months, we fought a hard campaign and took on a major local developer. It's up to us to keep up the momentum and challenge the unjust policies of the City of Vancouver and the BC Government that encourage developers like PortLiving to trample on tenants rights with impunity.[29]

VTU has a different origin story and footprint than FRAPRU and RCLALQ; it aims to support local groups and create an umbrella political movement simultaneously. The union is devoted to concrete, everyday struggles against abusive landlords, but also takes on the political class that defends elite interests at city hall and the provincial assembly. The latter includes producing research that challenges technocratic consensus.[30] It's a lot to take on, but subcommittees allow these efforts to happen in tandem. The steering committee works on coordination, while general assemblies serve as the democratic backbone. There are many strategies for building tenant power; the VTU model is ambitious, inspiring, and seems to work for Vancouver.

VTU's concern with supporting decolonization struggles also stands out. Its constitution states, "Decolonization is the end we are constantly working towards. As a mixed group of settlers and Indigenous peoples, we commit to examining our values, tactics and strategies to align with moves towards real, deep decolonizing work."[31] In one of the union's first general assembly meetings, members identified decolonization as a priority action area, with specify goals including "educate our members on decolonization, connect to local nations, and support the resurgence of Indigenous languages."[32] This priority is reiterated in *Basis for Unit*, a 2022 document that looks at the organization's first five years and articulates a way forward.[33]

In the opinion of one VTU organizer:

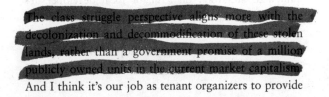

The class struggle perspective aligns more with the decolonization and decommodification of these stolen lands, rather than a government promise of a million publicly owned units in the current market capitalism

And I think it's our job as tenant organizers to provide

the necessary education to make that the accepted position in our movements.[34]

. . . AND MORE

Many other inspiring examples of tenant organizing in Canada were not mentioned here. Top of mind on the list of omissions are Toronto's Federation of Metro Tenants' Associations (FMTA) and Ottawa's Herongate Tenant Coalition. Founded in 1974, the FMTA is a coalition of tenant associations similar to Quebec's FRAPRU, or a long-established version of what the Vancouver Tenants Union is building. FMTA acts on three fronts: informing tenants about their rights and options, including offering a Tenant School Program; assisting tenant associations to form and challenge landlords on above-guideline rent increases (AGIs) and other struggles; and running advocacy campaigns. At the policy level, the organization has and continues to play a critical role in the political fights for rent controls.[35] On the ground, York South-Weston Tenant Union members referred to FMTA as an unwavering source of support.[36]

Herongate tenants have been fighting a courageous fight against one of the country's largest real estate investment firms, including filling a human rights case against "demoviction." In 2016, Hazelview demolished 83 rental townhouses in Ottawa's most diverse neighbourhood. In 2019, Hazelview came back for another 150 homes, and its new proposed redevelopment plans could lead to the demolition of another 559 houses.[37] The view of the Herongate Tenant Coalition is clear: "The only way to stop Hazelview's plans is for tenants to organize together, present demands as a group and refuse to move."[38]

In Winnipeg, the West Broadway Tenants Committee, launched only a year before the COVID-19 pandemic, has been finding ways to bring people together and fight AGIs despite lockdown measures that made organizing efforts more difficult. In their own words: "The Tenants Committee is a non-hierarchical, community-based group working towards building tenant power in West Broadway. Using a diverse range of actions and tactics, we operate explicitly in opposition to exploitative, negligent and absentee landlords and advocate for greater knowledge of specifics and deficiencies of the provincial Residential Tenancies Act."[39]

In Regina, the Queen City Tenants Association, active for several years in the 2010s, has recently gone dormant. Maybe it planted seeds that will sprout again. The Renters of Saskatoon Area also organize tenants in the province of Saskatchewan, using a human rights-based approach.

In Calgary, the Renters Action Movement has fought uphill battles, on and off, in a province without rent controls, in a city where homeownership is seen as almost inevitable. According to a local organizer, "it's really hard to achieve a critical mass and have anyone who wants to fight for renters' rights because there is that stigma attached to renting. Everybody's like, 'Why should I fight for renters if I'm going to buy a house eventually?'"[40] Despite uphill battles, the movement has played a crucial role in pushing for eviction bans at the beginning of the COVID-19 pandemic.[41] Edmonton has also seen efforts to organize a union named Edmonton Renters' Union, which seems to have been put on pause during the pandemic.

In Victoria, the Tenant Action Group is squarely focused on rental housing, like other tenant unions, but has a broader membership. It defines itself as:

> a membership-based organization committed to transforming the housing system and ensuring access to housing for all. Our members include tenants, co-op

residents, and people experiencing housing instability and homelessness. We work in solidarity with all people who do not own their homes and welcome the support of homeowners who share our vision for housing justice.[42]

The Association of Community Organizations for Reform Now (ACORN), Canada, is a multi-issue, membership-based group present in nine cities and twenty-four neighbourhoods across the country. It was founded in 2004 and modelled after the American organization with the same name. Although ACORN's campaigns focus on various issues that impact low-income families—including predatory lending, social assistance rates, child care fees, and internet access—most of its members are tenants, and housing issues have been the bedrock of its organizing efforts.[43]

Individual tenants also confront abusive landlords in the secondary rental market (condos, houses, triplex units, basements, rooms). Take Lucie's case, for example. She lived alone in a unit in Ottawa Centre for a few years. Upon receiving a job offer in Toronto, she gave notice to the landlord. The job offer was rescinded a few weeks later due to extenuating circumstances, but by then, the landlord had already planned to hike the rent by $250 (around 20 percent). There is no rent control on vacant units in Ontario, and units become technically vacant once notice is given, so he was allowed to require Lucie to pay that much more for staying put. She told him to shove it. After much looking, she found a recently built triplex unit on the Quebec side that fit her budget. After a year, the new landlord raised her rent by 8 percent. She asked why. "Because I can," he told her.

In Quebec, tenants do not have the right to contest rent

increases in units built within the past five years; they either accept the increase or move out. Lucie didn't have it in her to look for another place. On top of paying more, she is insecurely housed. She doesn't have the right to contest increases for another couple of years, and the landlord may raise the rent to more than she can afford because he can.[44]

Some tenants of isolated rental units join tenant groups, but most are on their own. Building broad tenant solidarity across individual tenant groups and the progressive movement writ large, and pushing for legislative changes, like rent controls, is particularly important for them.

———————

The historical and current stories of tenant struggles show the continued presence, geographical footprint, and political importance of tenant movements and the landlord class's readiness to squash tenant organizing efforts. Going back to before Confederation, during the inter-war and the Great Depression years, in the post-World War II period, during the heyday of urban renewal, and to this date, tenants have organized, fought landlords, and won important concessions from governments. They did so all over the country.

In most cases, landlords activate state protection; they send the cavalry after tenant groups, make them illegal, persecute their organizers, and instill fear in tenants as a way to break class consciousness. But landlords are never fully successful. Even when tenants are forced to retreat, organizing continues on other fronts and inspires future fights. Tenant-based class struggle is a part of this country's story, past and present.

There is a vertiginous disconnect between these class struggles carried out by organized tenants and housing debates among public policy experts, government officials, and much of the media. On the ground, it is clear that land-lords and tenants have conflicting interests: one side always has to give, and nobody wants to be on that side. In policy debates, technical language and crafted political communications conceal the fundamentally political and conflictual nature of housing issues. Public debate about housing assumes win-win solutions are possible. But if that's so, why haven't we found any definitive, win-win solution in the more than one hundred years we have talked about a "housing crisis" in Canada?

CHAPTER SIX

Pick a Side

There is no "housing crisis," just good old landlords squeezing high rents from tenants. The owning class gets rich on the back of working people. Laws allow it. Landlord and tenant boards enforce it. Cultural norms dictate that acquisition and speculation are worthy of praise, while renting past a certain age is frowned upon. Politicians respond accordingly, touting homeownership and turning their backs on tenants. Some media naively or disingenuously portrays landlords as struggling families trying to pay their mortgages. Policy wonks insist on referring to this situation as a "housing crisis," suggesting it requires technical solutions, whereas the problem is clearly political.

The challenge for the tenant class is not to *find* a solution for the so-called housing crisis but to *enact* the solutions we know work: move as much provision as possible outside of private markets; tightly regulate the remaining market provision; organize tenants to ensure quality and access. Easier said than done. The landlord class fights fiercely for its right to appropriate tenant income and turn it into personal wealth, and in doing so, it counts on the support of most of the political class. It takes political power to go up against the landlord class and force governments to rein in markets. But tenant movements already know this. They have known it for a long time.

Now, the question is where the rest of society stands, where you stand.

Free markets create wealth; take what it takes. Essential, life-supporting services are managed by governments, non-profit providers, co-operatives, tightly regulated markets, or a combination thereof. Most notably, hospitals and public schools are non-for-profit operations and universally accessible—and Canadians are proud of it. Public agencies and regulated companies also deliver water, recreation services, post-secondary education, and transit, among other things. There is a clear rationale for barring or regulating profit-making in these sectors: we want as many people as possible to access these basic services; if we allow markets to run wild, not everyone will be able to afford them. In turn, childcare and long-term care are examples of sectors where private and public services co-exist; there are ongoing disputes between those who want to make more room for private providers and those who want to regulate them out of business.

Then there are sectors where private markets hold the upper hand and public provision is marginal; examples include prescription drugs and rental housing. Eighty-eight percent of tenants are subject to the whims of the market. Only four of the ten provinces and three territories have rent controls on occupied units; only two have controls on vacant units. Even where rent controls exist, landlords can apply for exemptions. Why do landlords raise rents faster than inflation and wages? Because they can. Because governments allow them to. Because the property-owning class forged a long-lasting consensus against public housing.

Twenty years ago, Planning scholar David Hulchanski contended that keeping units off the market is the only way to protect low-rent housing. He added, "there is nothing new in this observation," then cited a 1948 book arguing the same.[1] The cited book, *Houses for Canadians*, by Humphrey Carver, then chair of the CMHC's Research Committee, revised tonnes of social, economic, and housing construction data, some of it going back to the beginning of the century. Drawing on this data, Carver tackled the "supply-side" argument head on: "it would be foolish to imagine that the combined effect of all the known economies in production would be sufficient to invalidate the main conclusion at which we have arrived, namely that the economic market cannot by itself fulfil the housing needs of the Canadian people."[2]

Seventy-five years ago, a detailed study by CMHC's research chair unambiguously stated private markets can't, won't solve Canada's housing issues. Yet, today all major official housing strategies in the country consist largely of providing ever more favourable conditions for private investors, developers, and landlords. It is not that governments lack ideas. Politicians just don't want to implement them, because doing so would hurt a parasitic but powerful economic elite.

Everyone who cares about rental housing has a choice to make: participate in the depoliticized and depoliticizing "housing crisis" debate or join the struggle against the landlord class and everyone defending its interests.

"Housing crisis" debates focus on technical solutions, policy tweaks, half measures. In an eternal search for elusive win-win solutions, policy analyses compare the outcomes of different policies and investments. Experts deliberate on trade-offs, argue about what is important, what is urgent, and what is an acceptable timeframe. In these contexts, words like profit and conflict are absent, deliberately avoided. Instead, it is common to hear things like "policy is the art of the possible," "this is too much to ask of this government," and "we should take whatever we can get." The level of self-censoring in these circles is high—to say the least. The willingness to compromise in the name of a false sense of pragmatism is astonishing. Once the "innovative" or "transformative" approach of the day proves unsuccessful, the specialists move on to the new policy fad—the policy merry-go-round.

In contrast, class-based demands are stubbornly intransigent. They are not solutions to policy puzzles but responses to historical oppression, not of any individual but an entire class. Try asking a tenant union member if they need a home with rent they can afford or one without pests. They will say both. And they need it now, not "over the next ten years." Likewise, the only reasonable rent increase is no increase at all. Rents take too much of families' incomes; they have to go down, not up. What maintenance problem should be addressed first? *All of them.* Landlords do not accept partial rent payments, so there should not be partially functioning units. Ask tenant organizers when it is acceptable to evict a tenant family that is struggling financially, and the answer will always be *never.* In class struggle, there are no half measures. No win-win solutions. You have to pick a side.

For those willing to do so, there are many ways to get involved. The direct way is to join or start a tenant union. Even in places without a city-wide tenant movement, solidarity between tenant groups exists, and experienced organizers assist incipient groups. At the time of writing, there are about 40 tenant unions in Canada with an online presence that could serve as the first point of contact to anyone trying to get started. In places like Montreal, Vancouver, and Victoria, tenants can join city-wide movements and then learn about ways to participate in or initiate local organizing. In Toronto, the Federation of Metro Tenants' Associations (FMTA) assists tenants trying to set up an association. Tenant resource and advocacy centres can also be starting points. They mostly focus on assisting individual cases rather than collective actions, but staff are knowledgeable and well connected to communities.

For people who are already part of class-based movements, it may simply be a matter of helping to bring tenant issues to the fore. This is particularly the case for the labour movement. Labour unions could play an enormously important role in supporting the tenant movement, as they have in the past, but that is not happening currently, not in any substantive and sustained manner. A large share of working-class boomers have become homeowners, but as that becomes less and less common, larger and larger shares of hard-fought-for wages will end up in the hands of landlords. For unionized and non-unionized workers in low-wage industries, that has been the case for a long time.

Researchers can play a supporting role, as long as our work is *for* and not *about* tenant movements. Research that advances knowledge and research careers is not necessarily helpful to political struggle. Too often, tenants are the subject but not the intended audience of research. Researchers seek to answer questions about tenants and tenant groups that will be of interest to academics, policy wonks, and the media but which tenants themselves may not have any use for. There is an easy way around this problem: ask organizers what they need, and do just that.

Then there is the policy crowd. There is a time and place for accepting to operate within the political constraints of the day and conducting problem-solving analysis. But when that is all we do, we become part of the problem. In my experience in policy circles in Canada, inside and outside of government, housing experts are too willing to accept those constraints, and rarely focus on stretching the realm of the possible. In this sphere, picking the side of tenants means challenging the elite-forged consensus against public housing at every opportunity. It means not assuming profit has to be part of the equation. It means giving up on elusive win-win solutions.

Journalists are bound to reporting the various sides of a story, but those sides should be depicted accurately. Most landlords are not families struggling to pay their mortgage or "mom and pop" landlords; they are wealthy families, profitable businesses, and aggressive investors. On the other side, an increasing number of tenants fighting abusive landlords are part of tenant movements that grow in numbers and strength every day, but news stories insist on portraying tenants as individuals fighting a lonely battle. Reacting to one such story, Parkdale Community Legal Services' Cole Webber tweeted, "centering the story on one Davisville tenant and a few tenant advocates when there are hundreds of tenants actively organizing against AGIs in Thorncliffe Park right now is a decision." Journalists may not be able to pick a side but they can make better decisions.

Every effort matters. Every abusive rent increase represents not only a landlord trying to squeeze money from a tenant but the landlord class appropriating income from working-class families, income that increases their wealth and influence, consolidating their ability to extract yet more income from yet more tenants. By the same token, every rent increase dropped, every stopped eviction, every repair completed, and every political win against landlords is a historic victory for the tenant class.

NOTES

INTRODUCTION: THE HOUSING CRISIS THAT ISN'T

1   Cited by Ontario Tenant Rights (website), ontariotenants.ca.

2   Douglas Marshall, "Tenant Power," *MacLean's*, April 1, 1969, macleans.ca.

3   "Des groups de locataires exigent la construction de nouveaux HLM," *Le Devoir*, April 19, 1980, 4.

4   As quoted in Jesse Donaldson, "Vancouver's 128 Years of Affordability Fears," *The Tyee*, November 24, 2012, thetyee.ca.

5   Bok G. Jeong and Jungwon Yeo, "United Nations and Crisis Management," *Global Encyclopedia of Public Administration, Public Policy, and Governance*, ed. Ali Farazmand (London, UK: Springer, 2018): 6041–48.

6   Stijn Claessens and Ayhan Kose, "Financial Crises: Explanations, Types, and Implications," *IMF Working Papers* 13, no. 28 (2013): 3, imf.org.

7   Ricardo Tranjan, "Crisis? What Crisis? One of Canada's Largest Landlords Is Having a Profitable 2020," *National Observer*, November 20, 2020, nationalobserver.com; Statistics Canada, "Real Estate Agents and Brokers, 2020," *The Daily*, February 24, 2022, statcan.gc.ca; Harry Wahl, "Despite Turbulent 2020 Home Builder Profit Margins Rose," *CoConstruct* (blog), March 9, 2022, coconstruct.com.

8   David Macdonald, "Another Year in Paradise: CEO Pay in

2020" (Report, Canadian Centre for Policy Alternatives, 2022), policyalternatives.ca.

9   Statistics Canada, Table 98-10-0252-01, "Shelter-Cost-to-Income Ratio by Tenure: Canada, Provinces and Territories, Census Metropolitan Areas and Census Agglomerations," 2022, statcan.gc.ca.

10   Josh Ryan-Collins, *Why Can't You Afford a Home?* (Cambridge, UK: Polity Press, 2019).

11   Canada Mortgage and Housing Corporation, "Rental Market Survey Data," 2020, cmhc-schl.gc.ca.

12   Canada Mortgage and Housing Corporation, "Rental Market Report: Canada and Selected Markets," 2021, cmhc-schl.gc.ca.

13   Steve Pomeroy, "Want to Solve the Housing Crisis? Address Super-Charged Demand," *The Conversation*, November 25, 2021, theconversation.com.

14   For a progressive argument for "supply-side" measures, see Alex Hemingway, "Five Reasons Supply Matters to the Housing Crisis," *Policy Note* (blog), September 14, 2022, policynote.ca.

15   Robert W. Cox, "Social Forces, States and World Orders: Beyond International Relations Theory," *Millennium: Journal of International Studies* 10, no. 2 (1981): 128, doi: 10.1177/03058298810100020501.

ONE: TENANTS, A SOCIAL CLASS

1   City of Toronto, "TO Prosperity: Toronto Poverty Reduction Strategy" (Staff Report. EX9.5, October 9, 2015). The author was part of the policy team in charge of consultations and the development of the poverty reduction strategy; some of the observations are based on first-hand experience.

2   Paul Shaffer and Ricardo Tranjan, "What to Expect from Toronto's Poverty Reduction Strategy?," *Canadian Public Policy* 45, no. 4 (2019): 483–96, jstor.org.

3   Karl Marx, *Capital: An Abridged Edition* (Oxford, UK: Oxford University Press, 1995).

4   Prabhat Patnaik, "Notes on the Concept of Class," *Social Scientist* 29, no. 9–10 (2000): 11, doi: 10.2307/3517974.

5   For the conventional Marxian distinction between the tenant-landlord and the worker-capitalist relationships,

see Frederick Engels, *The Housing Question* (Co-operative Publishing Society of Foreign Workers, 1995 [1887]), 17.

6 Marx, *Capital*, 364.

7 Glen Sean Coulthard, *Red Skin, White Masks: Rejecting the Colonial Politics of Recognition* (Minneapolis: University of Minnesota Press, 2014), 9.

8 Humphrey Carver, *Houses for Canadians: A Study of Housing Problems in the Toronto Area* (Toronto: University of Toronto Press, 1948).

9 Marc Lee, "Vacancy Control: Taking the Next Step on Housing Affordability," *Policy Note* (blog), February 11, 2021, policynote.ca.

10 Jennifer Y. Tsao, "How to Increase Affordable Rental Units in BC," *Intelligence Memos* (blog), August 10, 2016, cdhowe.org.

11 Ricardo Tranjan, Garima Talwar Kapoor, and Hannah Aldridge, "Locked Down, Not Locked Out: An Eviction Prevention Plan for Ontario," *The Monitor*, May 28, 2020, monitormag.ca.

12 Emily Mathieu, "How Much Do Canadians Spend on Rent? Ontario 'Hit Harder Than Anywhere Else' Says New Housing Tool," *Toronto Star*, September 17, 2019, thestar.com.

13 City of Toronto, "HousingTO 2020–2030 Action Plan," 2019, 10, toronto.ca.

14 City of Toronto, "HousingTO 2020–2030 Action Plan," 46.

15 Government of Canada, "National Housing Strategy: A Place to Call Home," 2017, publications.gc.ca.

16 Government of Canada, "National Housing Strategy," 15.

17 Government of Canada, "National Housing Strategy," 15.

18 Canada Mortgage and Housing Corporation, "Solutions Labs: Solving Complex Housing Problems Together," cmhc-schl.gc.ca.

19 Statistics Canada, Table 34-10-0133-0, "Canada Mortgage and Housing Corporation, Average Rents for Areas with a Population of 10,000 and Over," February 21, 2022, statcan.gc.ca; Statistics Canada, Table 18-10-0004-13, "Consumer Price Index by Product Group, Monthly, Percentage Change, Not Seasonally Adjusted, Canada, Provinces, Whitehorse, Yellowknife and Iqaluit," October 19, 2022, statcan.gc.ca; calculations by the author. For a

more accurate comparison, I excluded the shelter cost component of the inflation calculation and used the provincial inflation rate.

20 Canadian Mortgage and Housing Corporation, "Real Median Household Income (After-Tax), by Tenure, 2006-2019," April 28, 2021, cmhc-schl.gc.ca; Statistics Canada, Table 18-10-0004-13, "Consumer Price Index"; calculations by the author.

21 Canadian Mortgage and Housing Corporation, "Rental Market Report: Canada and Selected Markets," 2022, 10.

22 David Macdonald, "Unaccommodating: Rental Housing Wage in Canada" (Report, Canadian Centre for Policy Alternatives, 2019), policyalternatives.ca.

23 Ricardo Tranjan, "The Rent Is Due Soon: Financial Insecurity and COVID-19" (Report, Canadian Centre for Policy Alternatives, 2020), policyalternatives.ca.

24 The study zoomed in on the 3.4 million tenant households across Canada whose primary source of income is either wages and salaries or self-employment. Liquid assets included money in regular bank accounts, tax-free savings accounts, and non-registered financial investments (mutual funds, bonds, stocks, income trusts, and other investments). It did not include registered retirement savings plans, which are taxable at a high rate, often partially or entirely locked-in, and overall harder to access. It also does not include property (e.g., a vehicle).

TWO: MYTHS ABOUT THE TENANT CLASS

1 Darrell Bricker, "Six in Ten (63%) Canadians Who Don't Own a Home Have 'Given Up' on Ever Owning One," *Ipsos News*, April 29, 2022, ipsos.com.

2 Garry Marr, "Chasing the Canadian Dream: The Real Force Driving the Housing Boom in Our Big Cities," *Financial Post*, February 17, 2017, financialpost.com.

3 Justin Trudeau (@JustinTrudeau), on August 28, 2021.

4 Ricardo Tranjan, "Platform Crunch: Parties Don't Get It—Renting Is Not a Phase," *The Monitor*, September 7, 2021, monitormag.ca.

5 Statistics Canada, "The Dream of Homeownership Remains

Strong in Canada, Despite Record-High Housing Prices,"
StatsCan Plus, February 22, 2022, statcan.gc.ca.

6   Statistics Canada, Table 98-10-0252-01, "Shelter-Cost-to-
Income Ratio by Tenure."

7   Paulo Freire, *Pedagogy of the Oppressed* (New York, NY:
Continuum, 1970).

8   Nancy Fraser and Axel Honneth, *Redistribution or
Recognition? A Political-Philosophical Exchange* (Brooklyn,
NY: Verso, 2003), 23.

9   Charles Lammam and Hugh MacIntyre, "Increasing the
Minimum Wage in Ontario: A Flawed Anti-Poverty Policy,"
Fraser Research Bulletin, June 19, 2018, fraserinstitute.org.

10   David Macdonald, "Ontario Needs a Raise: Who Benefits
From a $15 Minimum Wage?" (Report, Canadian Centre for
Policy Alternatives, 2017), policyalternatives.ca.

11   Statistics Canada, Table 98-10-0232-01, "Age of Primary
Household Maintainer by Tenure: Canada, Provinces
and Territories, Census Metropolitan Areas and Census
Agglomerations," 2022, statcan.gc.ca.

12   Angus Reid Institute, "To Have & Have Not: Canadians
Take Sides on Housing Market, Divided in Desire for Home
Prices to Rise, or Tank," April 7, 2021, 20, angusreid.org.

13   Noah Smith, "Millennials Can't Afford Homes after
Exiting the Basement," *Bloomberg News*, July 24, 2020,
bloomberg.com.

14   Shazia Nazir, "Canadian Dream Slipping Out of Reach for
Young Families as Housing Crisis Looms," *Toronto Star*,
September 17, 2021, thestar.com.

15   Statistics Canada, "To Buy or to Tent: The Housing Market
Continues to be Reshaped by Several Factors as Canadians
Search for an Affordable Place to Call Home," *The Daily*,
September 21, 2022, statcan.gc.ca.

16   Canadian Mortgage and Housing Corporation,
"Homeownership Rates Varies Significantly by Race,"
Research Insight, November 2021, cmhc-schl.gc.ca.

17   Mike Chopowick, "The Rent Is Too Damn High (and
City Taxes Are to Blame)," *Federation of Rental-Housing
Providers of Ontario*, October 15, 2015.

18   City of Toronto, "2020 City Budget," 2020, toronto.ca.

19   Matt Elliott, "The Mathematical Truth about Toronto

Property Taxes: Raising Them Is the Best Option," *Toronto Star*, December 9, 2019, thestar.com.

20 Aaron A. Moore and R. Michael McGregor, "The Representativeness of Neighbourhood Associations in Toronto and Vancouver," *Urban Studies* 58, no. 13 (2021): 2782–97, doi: 10.1177/0042098020964439.

21 Statistics Canada, 2016001, "2016 Census (Public Use Microdata File)," 2019, statcan.gc.ca; calculations by the author.

22 Statistics Canada, Table 46-10-0047-01, "Total Income and Characteristics of Owners and Tax Filers Who Do Not Own Residential Property," 2022, open.canada.ca.

23 Statistics Canada, "Canadian Housing Survey: Public Use Microdata File, 2018," 2021, statcan.gc.ca; calculations by the author.

24 Statistics Canada, "2016 Census (Public Use Microdata File)."

25 Statistics Canada, "Survey of Financial Security: Public Use Microdata File, 2019," 2021, statcan.gc.ca; calculations by the author.

26 Statistics Canada, "Survey of Financial Security."

27 Statistics Canada, "Canadian Housing Survey."

28 Rob Carrick, "Renters, Here Are Seven Financial Advantages Over Homeowners," *Globe and Mail*, June 9, 2021, theglobeandmail.com.

29 Interview with Ayse Comeau, member-organizer of the Manor Park Tenant Union, June 2022.

30 Taylor Blewett, "Manor Park Redevelopment Application Brings Intensification, Displacement, Community Benefits Discussion to Planning Committee," *Ottawa Citizen*, March 9, 2022, ottawacitizen.com.

31 Blewett, "Manor Park."

32 Blewett, "Manor Park."

33 Learn more at facebook.com/ManorParkTenantUnion/.

34 Though not a direct reference, the author owes this insight to James Wilt, *Do Androids Dream of Electric Cars? Public Transit in the Age of Google, Uber, and Elon Musk* (Toronto: Between the Lines, 2020).

35 See, for example, Nemoy Lewis, "The Uneven Racialized Impact of Financialization: A Report for the Office of the

Federal Housing Advocate" (Report, Canadian Human Rights Commission, 2022), rondpointdelitinerance.ca.

THREE: BUT WHAT ABOUT THE LANDLORDS?

1   Ricardo Tranjan, "The Rent Is Due Soon: Financial Insecurity and COVID-19" (Report, Canadian Centre for Policy Alternatives, 2020).

2   Ricardo Tranjan, "L'annulation des loyers: un débat incontournable," *Policy Options*, April 15, 2020, policyoptions.irpp.org.

3   For a summary of existing datasets and data gaps, see Michelle Verbeek and Cynthia Belaskie, "Canadian Rental Market Data Sources," *Affordable Housing Monitor*, Canadian Housing Evidence Collaborative, 2021.

4   OECD, *Affordable Housing Database*, 2021, oecd.org.

5   Canada Mortgage and Housing Corporation, "Social and Affordable Housing Survey—Rental Structures," November 30, 2021, cmhc-schl.gc.ca; Statistics Canada, Table 98-10-0239-01, "Structural Type of Dwelling by Tenure: Canada, Provinces and Territories, Census Metropolitan Areas and Census Agglomerations," September 21, 2022, statcan.gc.ca. This calculation excludes social and affordable units where market prices are use as a determining mechanism. A very similar estimate is found in Statistics Canada, "Housing Challenges Remain for Vulnerable Populations in 2021," *The Daily*, July 7, 2021, statcan.gc.ca.

6   The discrepancy is due, at least in part, to the fact that OECD data exclude units managed by the Société d'habitation du Québec (SHQ).

7   "OECD Questionnaire on Affordable and Social Housing (QuASH)," oecd.org.

8   Greg Suttor, *Still Renovating: A History of Canadian Social Housing Policy* (Montreal: McGill-Queen's University Press, 2016).

9   Statistics Canada, "Canadian Housing Survey."

10 Suttor, *Still Renovating*.

11 Statistics Canada, "Canadian Housing Survey."

12 Based on the author's first-hand experience in community consultations in Toronto.

13 Michelle Cheung, "Toronto Community Housing: Thousands

of Units Could Close Due to Lack of Cash for Repairs," *CBC News*, March 11, 2016, cbc.ca; Natalie Johnson, "TCHC Buildings to Be Demolished, Rebuilt in Planned Queen-Coxwell Revitalization," *CTV News*, October 28, 2019, toronto.ctvnews.ca.

14   Statistics Canada, "Housing Challenges Remain for Vulnerable Populations in 2021."

15   Statistics Canada, "Canadian Housing Survey."

16   Roger D. Lewis, "A Profile of Purpose-Built Rental Housing in Canada" (Report, Canada Mortgage and Housing Corporation, 2016). In this widely cited analysis, Lewis includes publicly initiated and subsidized units as part of the secondary market. In everyday parlance, public housing is not always thought of as part of the secondary market, but it is in Lewis's estimates. The 38 percent estimate is based on his findings. For corroboration, I contrasted 2021 CMHC rental unit counts (RMS and RRMS) with 2021 Census data to estimate the share of tenant households that can be housed in purpose-built structures (of three units and over, in geographies of 2,500 people and more); my findings very closely matched Lewis's earlier estimates.

17   Statistics Canada, "Survey of Financial Security."

18   In Vancouver, for example, the median assessment value of the home of a single-property owner is $936,000, compared to $1,220,000 for two-property owners, $1,410,000 for three-property owners, and $1,570,000 for four-or-more-property owners; see Ellen Bekkering, Jean-Philippe Deschamps-Laporte and Marina Smailes, "Residential Property Ownership: Real Estate Holdings by Multiple-Property Owners," *Housing Statistics in Canada*, September 27, 2019, statcan.gc.ca.

19   Marg Bruineman, "Pandemic Creating a 'Nightmare' for Local Landlords and Tenants," *Toronto Star*, December 22, 2020, thestar.com.

20   Bruineman, "Pandemic Creating a 'Nightmare' for Local Landlords and Tenants."

21   According to Statistics Canada, "Survey of Financial Security," 4 percent of all homeowners in Canada rent a section of their only house. This figure, however, includes basements, which are increasingly treated as a second

home and a mechanism for wealth creation. The share of homeowners who take in boarders and housemates is even smaller. For an analysis of basements units, see Greg Suttor, "Basement Suites: Demand, Supply, Space, and Technology," *The Canadian Geographer* 61, no. 4 (2017), 483–92.

22   Lewis, "A Profile of Purpose-Built Rental Housing in Canada."

23   Gustavo Durango, "Rental Ownership Structure in Canada," *Housing Market Insight* (Ottawa: Canada Mortgage and Housing Corporation, 2017). Since purpose-built units comprises roughly half of the market (see note 6), the shares presented in Durango's report were divided by two, with an adjustment made to account for the expansion of financial landlords (see note 33).

24   Durango, "Rental Ownership Structure in Canada."

25   This estimate uses average rents (all units) available on CMHC's Housing Market Information Portal, multiplied by the number of units on the average-size building, multiplied by 12 months.

26   Matthew Desmond, *Evicted: Poverty and Profit in the American City* (New York: Broadway Book, 2016).

27   Niels Veldhuis and Amela Karabegovic, "McGuinty Puts Thousands of Jobs at Risk with Planned Increase in Minimum Wage," *Fraser Institute*, April 1, 2009, fraserinstitute.org.

28   "Who's Who 2020," *Canadian Apartment*, August 7, 2020; "Top 10 in the Canadian Apartment Industry," *Canadian Apartment Who's Who 2015*, July 27, 2015.

29   Carla Wilson, "Starlight Buys Eight Victoria Rental Apartment Buildings," *Western Investor*, June 7, 2021, westerninvestor.com.

30   Judy Trinh, "Evicted Heron Gates Residents Launch Human Rights Complaint," CBC News Ottawa, April 03, 2019, cbc.ca.

31   Learn more at herongatetenants.ca

32   Ferrer Alexander, "The Real Problem with Corporate Landlords," *The Atlantic*, June 21, 2021, theatlantic.com.

33   I used multiple sources for this estimate. Durango, "Rental Ownership Structure in Canada," estimated that financial landlords owned 11 percent of the purpose-built units

in 2016; Martine August, "The Financialization of Multi-Family Rental Housing in Canada: A Report for the Office of the Federal Housing Advocate," (Report, Canadian Human Rights Commission, 2022), homelesshub.ca, estimated that financial landlords owned 20 percent of the purpose-built rental stock in 2021. I used the figures August complied, which shows that financial landlords owned at least 344,000 units in 2020–21, but for consistency with other estimates in this chapter, I used 2021 CMHC data tables (RMS and RRMS) as the universe, arriving at 15.5 percent, right in between Durango's and August's estimates. Using the approximation described in note 84, this estimate represents 8 percent of all rental units. Based on qualitative data, I assumed that the growth between Durango's estimate and mine happened at the detriment of small business who were bought out in recent years.

34 Leilani Farha, "Report of the Special Rapporteur on Adequate Housing as a Component of the Right to an Adequate Standard of Living, and on the Right to Non-Discrimination in This Context" (New York: United National Human Rights Council, 2017), digitallibrary.un.org.

35 For a summary of much of her findings to date, in a format that is more accessible than academic journals, see August, "The Financialization of Multi-Family Rental Housing in Canada."

36 Danielle Kubes, "What You Need to Know about REITs," *MoneySense*, December 1, 2019, moneysense.ca.

37 Martine August, "The Rise of Financial Landlords Has Turned Rental Apartments into a Vehicle for Profit," *Policy Options*, June 11, 2021, policyoptions.irpp.org.

38 August, "The Financialization of Multi-Family Rental Housing in Canada," 3.

39 Joanne Lee-Young, "Vancouver Real Estate: REITs Announce $292 Million Purchase of 15 Rental Apartment Buildings," *Vancouver Sun,* January 12, 2021, vancouversun.com; August, "The Rise of Financial Landlords."

40 "Who's Who 2020," *Canadian Apartment*, August 7, 2020; "Top 10 in the Canadian Apartment Industry," *Canadian Apartment Who's Who 2015*, July 27, 2015.

FOUR: A HISTORY OF STRUGGLE

1   Néstor Medina and Becca Whitla, "(An)Other Canada Is Possible: Rethinking Canada's Colonial Legacy," *Horizontes Decoloniales/Decolonial Horizons* 5 (2019): 13–42, jstor.org/stable/10.13169/decohori.5.issue-1.

2   Medina and Whitla, "(An)Other Canada Is Possible," 23.

3   "The Stormy Future of Canadian Liberalism: An Interview with Ian McKay, Canada's Renegade Historian of Liberalism," *The Breach*, October 13, 2021, breachmedia.ca.

4   For a nuanced version of this argument, see Alvin Finkel, "Competing Master Narratives of Post-War Canada," *Acadiensis* XXIX, no. 2 (Spring 2000): 188–204, jstor.org.

5   Catherine McIntyre, "Justin Trudeau's Plan to Make Housing Great Again," *Maclean's*, November 23, 2017, macleans.ca.

6   Zachary Spicer, "The Reluctant Urbanist: Pierre Trudeau and the Creation of the Ministry of State for Urban Affairs," *International Journal of Canadian Studies* 44 (2011): 185–99, erudit.org.

7   Spicer, "The Reluctant Urbanist."

8   Pierson Nettling, "Tenant Activism and the Demise of Urban Renewal: Tenants, Governance, and the Struggle for Recognition at Habitations Jeanne-Mance in Montreal," *Journal of Urban History* 48, no. 3 (2020): 2, doi: 10.1177/0096144220950672.

9   Nettling, "Tenant Activism and the Demise of Urban Renewal," 2.

10 A noteworthy example of this sort of study is Bryan D. Palmer and Gaétan Héroux, *Toronto's Poor: A Rebellious History* (Toronto: Between the Lines, 2016).

11 For an example related to housing struggles see, RCLALQ, "40 ans de luttes du RCLALQ pour le droit au logement 1978–2018," *RCLALQ* 2018, rclalq.qc.ca.

12 François Saillant, *Lutter pour un toit: Douze batailles pour le logement au Québec* (Montreal: Les Éditions Écosociété, 2018).

13 Yutaka Dirks, "Community Campaigns for the Right to Housing: Lessons from the R2H Coalition of Ontario," *Journal of Law and Social Policy*, 24 (2015): 135–42, osgoode.yorku.ca.

14 Learn more at righttoremain.ca.

15 Learn more at radicalhousingjournal.org.

16 Carolyn Taylor, "Our History, Our Stories: Personal Narratives and Urban Aboriginal History in Prince Edward Island" (Urban Aboriginal Knowledge Network, 2019), uakn.org.

17 Ian Ross Robertson, *The Tenant League of Prince Edward Island, 1864–1867: Leasehold Tenure in the New World* (Toronto: University of Toronto Press, 1996).

18 John I. Little, "Review of The Tenant League of Prince Edward Island, 1864–1867, by I. R. Robertson," *Labour / Le Travail* 42 (Fall 1998): 246–47, jstor.org; Matthew G. Hatvany, "The Tenant League of Prince Edward Island, 1864–1867: Leasehold Tenure in the New World," *The American Review of Canadian Studies* 28, no. 4 (Winter 1998): 563–65.

19 Robertson, *The Tenant League of Prince Edward Island 1864–1867*, 13.

20 Robertson, *The Tenant League of Prince Edward Island 1864–1867*, 19.

21 Robertson, *The Tenant League of Prince Edward Island 1864–1867*, 20.

22 Robertson, *The Tenant League of Prince Edward Island 1864–1867*, 64.

23 Barry Cahill, "The Halifax Relief Commission (1918–1976): Its History, Historiography, and Place in Halifax Disaster Scholarship," *Research Notes* 47, no. 2 (2019), erudit.org.

24 Suzanne Morton, "Men and Women in a Halifax Working-Class Neighbourhood in the 1920s" (PhD diss., Dalhousie University, 1990), 39.

25 Morton, "Men and Women in a Halifax Working-Class Neighbourhood in the 1920s," 32.

26 Ava Coulter, Isabel Ruitenbeek, and Julia-Simone Rutgers, "The Story of Turtle Grove," *The Signal*, December 6, 2017, signalhfx.ca.

27 As quoted in John C. Bacher, "From Study to Reality: The Establishment of Public Housing in Halifax," *Acadiensis* 18, (1988): 121, erudit.org.

28 Bacher, "From Study to Reality," 121.

29 Bacher, "From Study to Reality," 134.

30 John C. Bacher, "Canadian Housing 'Policy' in Perspective," *Urban History Review* 15, (June 1986), jstor.org.

31 See, for example, the comprehensive report by H. Peter Oberlander and Arthur L. Fallick, "Housing a Nation: The Evolution of Canadian Housing Policy" (The University of British Columbia: Centre for Human Settlements, 1992), publications.gc.ca; also, Paul Hellyer's Wikipedia page. While it may not be a creditable source, it is indicative of general knowledge. It states, "Grand urban renewal projects would come to an end as a result of his Task Force."

32 Nettling, "Tenant Activism and the Demise of Urban Renewal."

33 Nettling, "Tenant Activism and the Demise of Urban Renewal," 4.

34 Oberlander and Fallick, *Housing a Nation*, 86–87.

35 Nettling, "Tenant Activism and the Demise of Urban Renewal," 7.

36 Corporation d'habitation Jeanne-Mance, "Terre d'accueil," 2017.

37 Originally called the Vancouver Tenants Organizing Committee (VTOC).

38 Bruce Yorke, "The Tenant Movement in B.C. from 1968 to 1978," *The Mainlander*, November 9, 2012, themainlander.com.

39 Paul S. Jon, "Tenant Organizing and the Campaign for Collective Bargaining Rights in British Columbia, 1968–75," *BC Studies* 206 (Summer 2020), library.ubc.ca.

40 Yorke, "The Tenant Movement in B.C. from 1968 to 1978."

41 Yorke, "The Tenant Movement in B.C. from 1968 to 1978."

42 Yorke, "The Tenant Movement in B.C. from 1968 to 1978."

43 Yorke, "The Tenant Movement in B.C. from 1968 to 1978."

44 Suttor, *Still Renovating*, 83.

45 Alvin Finkel, *Social Policy and Practice in Canada: A History* (Waterloo: Wilfrid Laurier University Press, 2006), 237.

FIVE: TENANT ORGANIZING TODAY

1   This analysis does not include organizations that provide services to tenants and advocate on their behalf—like the Tenant Resource & Advisory Council (TRAC), Advocacy Centre for Tenants Ontario (ACTO), or the Canadian Centre

for Housing Rights (CCHC)—or right to housing advocacy networks—like The National Right to Housing. All of these organizations do invaluable work but they are not the focus of this particular study.

2   Interview with Bruno Dobrusin, member-organizer of the York South-Weston Tenant Union, November 2021.

3   Emily Power and Bjarke Skærlund Risager, "Rent-Striking the REIT: Reflections on Tenant Organizing Against Financialized Rental in Hamilton, Ontario, Canada," *Radical Housing Journal* 1, no. 2 (2019): 90, radicalhousingjournal.org. Author bios included in the article: Emily Power is a member of the Hamilton Tenants Solidarity Network (HTSN). Bjarke Skærlund Risager is a Postdoctoral Fellow in the Department of Geography & Planning, University of Toronto, and is doing participatory action research with HTSN.

4   Power and Risager, "Rent-Striking the REIT," 89.

5   Power and Risager, "Rent-Striking the REIT," 89–90.

6   Power and Risager, "Rent-Striking the REIT," 92.

7   Power and Risager, "Rent-Striking the REIT," 94.

8   Power and Risager, "Rent-Striking the REIT," 97.

9   Power and Risager, "Rent-Striking the REIT," 97–98.

10   Hamilton Tenants Solidarity Network, "Statement on the Dissolution of Hamilton Tenants Solidarity Network," *It's Going Down*, February 5, 2020, itsgoingdown.org.

11   Cole Webber and Ashleigh Doherty, "Staking Out Territory: District-Based Organizing in Toronto, Canada," *Radical Housing Journal* 3, no. 1 (2021): 230, radicalhousingjournal.org. Author bios included in the article: Cole Webber has been a legal aid worker in Parkdale for the past decade. He is a member of Parkdale Organize; Ashleigh Doherty has been a member of Parkdale Organize since it began seven years ago. She is a tenant in a MetCap building in Parkdale and teaches at a neighbourhood public school.

12   Webber and Doherty, "Staking Out Territory," 233.

13   Webber and Doherty, "Staking Out Territory," 241.

14   City of Toronto, "2016 Neighbourhood Profile, South Parkdale," 2018.

15   Carolyn Whitzman and Tom Slater, "Village Guetto Land: Myth, Social Conditions, and Housing Policy in Parkdale,

Toronto, 1879–2000," *Urban Affairs Review* 41, no. 5 (2006): 673–96, doi: 10.1177/1078087405284673.

16 Webber and Doherty, "Staking Out Territory," 235–38.

17 "Organize Tenants Stop Eviction," Parkdale Organize, January 9, 2021, parkdaleorganize.ca.

18 "Parkdale Tenants Beat Renovictions," Parkdale Organize, April 19, 2022, parkdaleorganize.ca.

19 "Statement of Principles," Parkdale Organize, parkdaleorganize.ca.

20 "About Us," York South-Weston Tenant Union, tenantunion.ca.

21 Written correspondence with York South-Weston Tenant Union organizers, December 2021.

22 Written correspondence with York South-Weston Tenant Union organizers, December 2021.

23 Interview with Bruno Dobrusin.

24 Interview with Chiara Padovani, member-organizer of the York South-Weston Tenant Union, December 2021.

25 RCLALQ, "40 ans de luttes du RCLALQ pour le droit au logement 1978–2018."

26 FRAPRU, "Historique," *Le Front d'action Populaire En Réaménagement Urbain*, frapru.qc.ca.

27 RCLALQ, "40 ans de luttes du RCLALQ pour le droit au logement 1978–2018," 13.

28 FRAPRU, "Dépliant le logement: pas une marchandise, un droit!," 2021, frapru.qc.ca.

29 Vancouver Tenants Union, "How We Won at Broadway-Carolina," *Vancouver Tenants Union*, January 18, 2021, vancouvertenantsunion.ca.

30 See, for example, Vancouver Tenants Union, "Renters Plan: An Alternative to Transit-Oriented Displacement Along Broadway," 2022, nationbuilder.com.

31 Vancouver Tenants Union, "Constitution of the Vancouver Tenants Union," vancouvertenantsunion.ca.

32 Vancouver Tenants Union, "April 2019 General Meeting," May 2019, vancouvertenantsunion.ca.

33 Vancouver Tenants Union, *Basis of Unity*, May 2022, nationbuilder.com.

34 Correspondence with Mazdak Gharibnavaz, VTU member-organizer, September 2, 2022.

35 According to more than one source, FMTA played a critical role in the successful fight for rent controls in the 1970s, but written accounts weren't found. Recently, the organization published a comprehensive review of rent control literature: see Phillip Mendonça-Vieira, "Actually, Rent Control Is Great" (Toronto: Federation of Metro Tenants' Associations, 2018).

36 Learn more at torontotenants.org.

37 Tammy Mast and Josh Hawley, "A Framework for Destruction: Hazelview and the City's Plan to Demolish 559 More Homes in Heron Gate Village," *The Leveller*, December 20, 2021, leveller.ca.

38 Learn more at herongatetenants.ca.

39 More about the West Broadway Tenant Union can be found in a Talking Radio interview, available at talkingradical.ca.

40 Ximena González, "Why Do Renters Get a Bad Rap in Calgary?," *The Sprawl*, May 22, 2021, sprawlcalgary.com.

41 Daniel Austin, "Alberta Assures Renters They Won't Be Evicted During COVID-19 Crisis," *Calgary Herald*, March 27, 2020, calgaryherald.com.

42 "Who We Are," Victoria Tenant Action Group, victoriatenants.com.

43 Learn more at acorncanada.org.

44 Interview with Lucie, June 15, 2022. Pseudonym used at interviewee's request.

SIX: PICK A SIDE

1   J. David Hulchanski, "Housing Policy for Tomorrow's Cities," Discussion Paper F|27 (Toronto: Canadian Policy Research Networks, 2002), utoronto.ca.

2   Carver, *Houses for Canadians*, 126.

INDEX

RICARDO TRANJAN is a political economist and senior researcher with the Canadian Centre for Policy Alternatives. Previously, Tranjan managed Toronto's Poverty Reduction Strategy and taught at universities in Ontario and Quebec. His early academic work focused on economic development and participatory democracy in Brazil, his native country. His current research is on the political economy of social policy in Canada. Ricardo holds a PhD from the University of Waterloo, where he was a Vanier Scholar. A frequent media commentator in English and French, he lives in Ottawa.